EVERYONE'S GUIDE TO
Hebrews

D1103661

Other books by Neil R. Lightfoot

How We Got the Bible

EVERYONE'S GUIDE TO
Hebrews

Neil R.
Lightfoot

Baker Books

A Division of Baker Book House Co
Grand Rapids, Michigan 49516

Published by Baker Books
a division of Baker Book House Company
P.O. Box 6287, Grand Rapids, MI 49516-6287

Printed in the United States of America

Library of Congress Cataloging-in-Publication Data

Lightfoot, Neil R.
    Everyone's guide to Hebrews / Neil R. Lightfoot.
        p.   cm.
    Includes bibliographical references.
    ISBN 0-8010-6420-1 (pbk.)
      1. Bible. N.T. Hebrews—Commentaries. I. Title.
    BS2775.53 .L54 2002
    227'.8707—dc21   2002009512

For current information about all releases from Baker Book House, visit our web site: http://www.bakerbooks.com

To
Kirby and Kaaren Barker
and
Dub and Polly Orr
who have perfected the gift of giving
without remembering it.

Contents

Preface

While I was in college as an undergraduate, a hard-nosed teacher made an unreasonable assignment. He required his students to memorize Hebrews. I was not in that class due to a schedule conflict, but I decided that if others could memorize Hebrews, so could I. At that time my study and love of Hebrews began, and it remains now many years later. Earlier, I had preached my first sermon on Hebrews 2:1–3, "The Great Salvation."

Of course, I could not envision then that it would be my privilege to teach Hebrews over many years to numerous graduate and undergraduate classes at Abilene Christian University. Nor did I think that I would often be speaking on it in Bible classes and in sermons. All of this has been for me a supreme joy.

This is now the second book I have written on Hebrews. It is entirely new and different. Its aim is to make the wonderful Book of Hebrews understandable for everybody.

I hasten to add that this book is not a commentary in the full sense of the term. On the other hand, as in a commentary, I have tried to make the meaning of the text stand out as clearly as possible. Hopefully, I have done this in an interesting and practical way. This has always been my goal in teaching.

This book is divided into fourteen chapters. If thirteen are preferred (e.g., for class use), I recommend combining chapters 9 and 10.

Many books and articles have helped me immeasurably on Hebrews, but in a work of this kind I cannot acknowledge them all. Some are listed in the "For Further Reading" section at the end of the book.

My sincere thanks go to many who have expressed their appreciation for my *Jesus Christ Today: A Commentary on the Book of Hebrews*. First published by Baker Book House, it has been reprinted by Bible Guides (P.O. Box 273, Abilene, Texas 79604). *Everyone's Guide to Hebrews* and *Jesus Christ Today* stand on their own, but here and there the former will augment the latter.

An alternate title for this book would be *Beautiful Savior*, taken from the beloved hymn, "Fairest Lord Jesus," because Hebrews marvelously describes and extols Jesus as the Beautiful Savior.

My hope is that *Everyone's Guide to Hebrews* will spur on more studies and classes in Hebrews, but I've written it especially to honor him who is our Beautiful Savior!

NEIL R. LIGHTFOOT
ABILENE CHRISTIAN UNIVERSITY
FEBRUARY 9, 2002

1

A Message of Exhortation

Bear with my word of exhortation.
HEBREWS 13:22

There is something about Hebrews that is appealing and beautiful. Its majestic language and style, its bold declarations, its sweeping arguments, its heartfelt pleas, all are without parallel in the New Testament. From a literary standpoint alone, it deserves the description "a little masterpiece." Its opening sentence well illustrates its magnificence: "In many and various ways God spoke of old to our fathers by the prophets, but in these last days he has spoken to us by a Son." Hebrews, to use another figure, is a work of art. As with Michelangelo's *Moses* and Raphael's *Transfiguration,* one senses the beauty of Hebrews at first sight.

But a work of art, to be fully appreciated, has to be studied. What is there to learn about its history and background? For whom was it produced, and why? Who was the artist that brought it forth and with what skill did he execute his work?

Hebrews as a masterpiece poses many questions. In a study of this kind, it is not possible to address all these questions. Yet some of the main ones must be dealt with, and, fortunately, a careful look at the work provides clues to the answers. Beyond its intriguing questions, Hebrews unfolds a remarkable message which seeks to be heard.

Chapter 13

How shall we start our study of Hebrews? Perhaps the best place to turn is chapter 13. This is a strange procedure, to begin at the end, but there are good reasons for doing so. First, chapter 1 is without an opening address, which normally would identify the author and the original readers. Second, chapter 13, as is often the case in the conclusion of Greek letters, preserves more of the historical circumstances of Hebrews than we can find elsewhere. Third, chapter 13 exhibits some of the main features of the book as a whole.

As we read chapter 13, here are some points that stand out about Hebrews.

1. *It is a letter*. Although Hebrews begins very much like a sermon, it clearly ends like a letter. In a typical Greek letter of the ancient world, greetings to other persons are included at the closing. This is why, for example, such a long list of names appears in Romans 16, where Paul sends his hearty greetings to many of his acquaintances. Hebrews likewise concludes with greetings (v. 24). Another element often included at the conclusions of such letters is

the benediction, and Hebrews is no exception (vv. 20–21). Still other features of ancient Greek letters which occur in Hebrews are travel plans and the closing farewell.

2. *It is a letter to a specific congregation.* We can see in Hebrews 13 that the author of Hebrews and the readers have close ties. He asks for their prayers (v. 18) and expects to see them soon (vv. 19, 23). He knows about their leaders, past and present (vv. 7, 17) and now extends greetings to their current leaders. The phrase "Greet all your leaders and all the saints" (v. 24) may well be a clue that Hebrews was written originally to a group of Christians who formed a house church. If not, why would the author say greet "all your leaders" and "all the saints"?

Other sections of Hebrews show clearly that it was a specific letter to a specific congregation with specific problems. The readers had suffered physical persecution; they had suffered the loss of property; yet they had stood the test well (10:32–34). Earlier chapters relate that they had learned the gospel from eye and ear witnesses of Christ (2:3), that they had been Christians for some time (5:12), and that they had been and were still active in serving their fellow Christians (6:10). Chapter 12 adds that, although they had undergone persecution, none of them had yet suffered martyrdom (12:4). All of this tells us that Hebrews was not a general letter, but was a letter sent to a particular congregation with a glorious past.

3. *It is a letter of exhortation.* Again, this is plain in chapter 13. As the author concludes his message, he says: "I urge you to bear with my word of exhortation" (v. 22 NIV). Chapter 13, from verse 1 on, contains exhortation after exhortation. Similar exhortations interlace the entire letter. Some are short and to the point, while others are much lengthier and combine a variety of admonitions with expositions of selected passages from the Old Testament. Here are the exhortations in Hebrews:

2:1–4: Exhortation against **d**rifting from God's word

3:7–4:16: Exhortation against **d**isbelieving God's word

5:11–6:20: Exhortation against **d**ullness toward God's word

10:19–13:25: Exhortation to **d**raw near to God

Of the 305 verses in Hebrews, 172 are exhortation verses. This means that more than half of Hebrews consists of special appeals to its readers.

Hebrews, then, is the *longest sustained exhortation for Christians to hold on to their faith.* Is a study of Hebrews important? Just as important as it is for you and me to hold on to our faith! "You have need of endurance," the author says (10:36). Abraham "patiently endured," awaiting God's promise (6:15). Moses, after his escape from Egypt and through long years in Midian, "endured as seeing him who is invisible" (11:27). And Christ had to "endure" the cross (12:2). Hold on, do not give up, go forward in the Christian pathway—this is the plea of Hebrews. Whatever else we may have thought Hebrews to be, it is truly "a message of exhortation."

4. It is a letter of warning. The exhortations in Hebrews contain solemn warnings. Chapter 13, again, well illustrates this. In verses 7–9 the author says, in effect, "Remember your leaders who first preached the gospel to you. That gospel has not changed, for Jesus Christ is always the same. So do not be led away by strange teachings."

Here we have exhortation and warning, a pattern noticeable throughout Hebrews. Years had passed since the first readers of this letter had become Christians. Enthusiasm among them was dying out, and some especially were in serious danger. "By this time you ought to be teachers, [yet] you need some one to teach you again" (5:12). "Take care . . . lest there be in any of you an evil, unbelieving heart" (3:12). "How shall we escape if we neglect such a great salvation?" (2:3).

In addition, there are the somber warnings in 6:4–8 and in 10:26–31, with the latter concluding in the words, "It is a fearful thing to fall into the hands of the living God." And yet, time and again, the author encourages with his often-repeated words, "let us." "Let us fear lest" (4:1; also 4:11, 14, 16). "Let us . . . go on to maturity" (6:1). "Let us draw near" (10:22). "Let us run with perseverance" (12:1). "Let us be grateful" (12:28).

5. *It is a letter of doctrinal significance.* In chapter 13, immediately after the author warns against false teaching, he declares that Christians "have an altar," which others have no right to partake of (v. 10). That altar, as the context makes clear, stands figuratively for the sacrifice of Christ. Only Christians benefit from his once-offered, sacrificial blood. By this the author not only sums up much of what he has previously said, but he focuses on the unforgettable difference that Christ makes for all of us. So Hebrews is not just exhortations and warnings. It is much more than a pep talk. Almost half of Hebrews concerns Christ and what he has accomplished and the eternal significance of it. This is the solid foundation the author lays for his warnings and encouragements.

Unanswered Questions

Although chapter 13 supplies much helpful information on Hebrews, there are many questions that it cannot answer. We would like to know more, and on some points all thirteen chapters leave us tantalizingly in the dark. Who was the author of Hebrews, and why did he not name himself? Where was he when he wrote, and when did he write? And where did these early Christians live who first received this letter?

On the question of authorship, many people believe that Hebrews is the work of Paul. The title in the King James Version reads: "The Epistle of Paul the Apostle to the Hebrews." Yet this is only a traditional title and is not found in the earliest manuscripts. Perhaps Paul wrote Hebrews, perhaps he did not. What is important is the *authority* with which the author wrote. His very manner and tone, his close connections with the church he addressed, and the contents of his message, all argue that he wrote as a recognized Christian teacher inspired by God's Spirit.

As to when the author wrote, it seems reasonable to suppose a date prior to the destruction of Jerusalem in A.D. 70. When we read that Levi "receives tithes" (7:9) and of others who "serve the tent" (13:10), such expressions argue, though not conclusively, that worship is still going on in the Jerusalem temple.

Concerning the original readers of Hebrews and where they lived, nothing is definitely known. "Those from Italy" (13:24) implies either that the author or the readers were in Italy. Because this letter is known as "Hebrews," a number of people believe that the readers addressed were living in Jerusalem or in Palestine. But this claims more than the title says, and no evidence otherwise occurs in the letter to support this view.

We may ask why this letter has come to be known so generally as "Hebrews." We know that this title goes at least as far back as the end of the second century, and we know also that the simple title "To Hebrews" is the earliest title in the extant Greek manuscripts. Probably the title was assigned to the letter because it seems to be written to Christians of Jewish background. The letter is filled with references to the Jewish form of worship—the tabernacle, the priesthood, the sacrifices, and all that went with them. Nothing here speaks to people of pagan background. Further, the entire argument of the letter is that the Old Testament, with its institutions and promises, finds its full meaning only in Christ. This is the very kind of argument that might be expected for those who were first nurtured in the Jewish faith.

Purpose

If indeed Hebrews was at first directed to Jewish Christians, what was it that made their situation peculiar and vulnerable to temptation? Let us try to imagine what it was like. On one hand was the land promised to the fathers, with Jerusalem, the city of David, as its center. The Jew could travel to Jerusalem and see with his own eyes the illustrious temple, hear the beautiful music, smell the sweet incense, and watch the priests with their impressive offerings. On the other hand was the worship of Christians in private homes—no priests, no sacrifices, no pageantry to glory in. Besides, there were the Gentiles crowding into the churches with no regard for the time-honored traditions of the fathers. What was going to happen next? Yes, Jesus had been preached and had been received by many Jews. But had he restored the kingdom to Israel (cf. Acts 1:6)? Why had he delayed so long in his coming?

From the contents of the letter, it seems that the purpose of Hebrews is to encourage the readers to make an ultimate choice between Judaism and Christianity. Were they teeter-tottering between the two? If so, this is why the author urges them so stringently to hold on to the Christ they have confessed (3:1; 4:14; cf. 3:6, 14; 10:23). Were they dangerously close to a complete relapse into Judaism? If so, this is why the author maintains that to reject Christ, to trample him underfoot and disdain his blood (10:26–29), is the same as to crucify him again, with irrevocable consequences (6:4–6). Either way, the exhor-

tation is to go to Christ "outside the camp" (13:13), bearing the stigma that was his. That is, go to Christ regardless
of the outcome, for to fall back from him is to reject the
only way that leads to life.

As a lawyer is:
"speaking passionately on your
Vocabulary   *beliefs"*

A particular word now needs to be said about the special language of Hebrews. In many respects Hebrews is
very different from other books of the New Testament. Its
message, centered in Christ as Savior, wonderfully com-
plements the New Testament message as a whole. But one
cannot read through Hebrews without being struck with
its distinctiveness. It is a "message of exhortation" some-
what along the lines of a homily or sermon (cf. Acts 13:15),
and it reads to some extent like an oral address. (As you
study Hebrews, read it *aloud* and take the time to *listen* to
its message.) It makes frequent reference to "speaking"
(2:5; 5:11; 6:9; 9:5; cf. 11:32); its language is rhetorical
and highly literary.

Aside from its literary qualities, the vocabulary of
Hebrews is quite different. This is perhaps the main reason why so many people find Hebrews hard to understand, for it is a difficult book unless one gets acquainted
with its unusual stock of terms. Three features should be
kept in mind about the language of Hebrews.

1. It is language steeped in the Old Testament. The very
framework of Hebrews consists of practical expositions
of selected Old Testament texts. This can be sketched out
as follows:

Hebrews Chapters	Old Testament References
1	7 OT quotations
2	Ps. 8; Ps. 22; Isa. 8

3	Num. 12; Ps. 95
4	Ps. 95; Gen. 2
5	Ps. 2; Ps. 110
6	Allusions to OT
7	Gen. 14; Ps. 110
8	Jer. 31
9	Allusions to OT
10	Ps. 40; Jer. 31; Hab. 2
11	Allusions to OT
12	Prov. 3; Hag. 2
13	Ps. 118

In all, Hebrews contains about thirty quotations from the Old Testament and about seventy allusions to it.

2. It is language of ritual and ceremony. This is true because Hebrews has so much to do with "sacrifices" and "offerings" and "priests." Indeed, Hebrews abounds in priestly terminology—"draw near" as an Old Testament priest would approach God in performing his priestly service; "perfect" in the sense of consecrating a priest to his office; "sanctify" to mean "make holy" in God's sight; "minister" to refer to a priestly minister; and so forth.

3. It is language of comparison and analogy. There is the speaking of the prophets and the speaking of the Son (1:1–2); the message declared by angels and the great salvation declared by the Lord (2:2–3); the glory of man and the glory of Jesus (2:7–9); the rest in Canaan and the rest in heaven (4:1–13); Aaron as high priest and Jesus as high priest (5:1–10); the blood of goats and calves and the blood of Christ (9:12–14). On and on it goes, language of contrast and comparison.

It is here where many readers of Hebrews stumble. They never quite understand that there is much in Hebrews which cannot be taken literally. Hebrews 6:19–20 says that Jesus has gone "behind the curtain." This, of course, is language of analogy. In the earthly tabernacle the Holy of Holies was set off by a curtain. Christ has gone, so to speak, into the heavenly Holy of Holies beyond the curtain. In Hebrews 8:2 and 9:11, the "true tent" and "the greater and more perfect tent" do not refer to a tent at all. There is no "tent" in heaven, but such language is determined by the analogy required. Nor did Christ "take" his own blood into heaven. Rather, he entered the heavenly Holy Place, right where God is, and there, so to speak, he sprinkled his own blood and obtained eternal redemption (9:12).

All of this means that special care must be given to the vocabulary of Hebrews. It is beautiful, complex, and subtle. The author's style is highly rhetorical and possesses poetic qualities. As it is said,

> A poet one can only rightly understand
> When one goes into the poet's land.

Anyone who does not remember this is destined to misunderstand Hebrews.

Christ the Center

Even though Hebrews takes its terminology from an ancient world of ceremony, still it must be kept in mind that Hebrews especially exalts Christ. He is above all. He is the heart and center of Hebrews.

It is to the author's lasting credit that he begins Hebrews at the center, not at the circumference. God has spoken his final message through one who is Son. The author does not focus attention on his readers. He does not begin with their problems or urge them to share their problems with others. He knows that what they need is Christ. If only they can come to a full appreciation of him, if only they can truly recognize what he has done for them, then they can successfully deal with their congregational and personal problems, whatever they are. "Fix your thoughts on Jesus," he says, "the apostle and high priest" whom we have confessed (3:1 NIV). This was their supreme need. It is our need today. The message of the uniqueness of Christ is always relevant.

Hebrews arranges all of its leading ideas around two great themes: the person of Christ and the work of Christ. The first part of Hebrews concerns *who* Christ is, the last part *what* Christ does. Broadly speaking, Hebrews can be outlined as follows:

Chapters 1–6: the word of God—who Christ is
Chapters 7–10: the work of God—what Christ does
Chapters 11–13: the word of God—concluding exhortations

Who is this Christ? In chapters 1–6 we see him as the Son of God. As Son he is greater than the prophets (1:1) and greater than the angels (1:2–2:18). As Son he is greater than Moses (3:1–6), greater than Joshua (4:1–10), and greater than Aaron (5:1–10).

What has this Christ done? In chapters 7–10 we see him as Son and priest. Actually, the priesthood of Jesus is alluded to and even stated plainly in the early chapters as well (1:3; 2:17; 4:14–5:10). If chapter 1 depicts him as Son of God, chapter 2 presents him as Son of Man. The Son, made like his brothers (2:17), clothed himself in a human body (2:14). He became, for a little while, lower than the angels (2:9). He accepted the human condition, including the painful stress of temptation (2:18; 4:15). Son though he was, he learned obedience, all the way to the cross; and having learned this final lesson, he is qualified to be our high priest (5:8–9). Indeed, his death on the cross was a high-priestly act (cf. 8:3). Historically, it took place on earth, "outside the city gate" (13:12 NIV), but on earth he could not be high priest (8:4). Therefore, his great high-priestly act, the sacrifice of himself, belongs to heaven. There, figuratively, he sprinkled his own blood before God as an eternal offering (9:12–14). There, in heaven—where there are no shadows (cf. 10:1)—the *real* sacrifice was made. It is no wonder that God crowned him with glory and honor (2:9).

> Beautiful Savior! Lord of all nations!
> Son of God and Son of Man.
> Glory and Honor, Praise, adoration
> Now and forever more be thine.

QUESTIONS

1. Why should we begin a study of Hebrews with chapter 13? What are some of the main points we learn from its closing verses?
2. From chapter 13 and elsewhere, show how Hebrews is a letter written to a definite congregation?
3. How is Hebrews both a "word of exhortation" and a letter of warning? Discuss and illustrate this by reference to specific passages.
4. What can we learn from the letter about the original readers of Hebrews? What do we know about their past experiences and their present problems? In light of this information, discuss the overall purpose of the letter.
5. What is distinctive about the vocabulary of this letter? Why is it important to pay attention to this?
6. In a preliminary way, show how Christ is the center of Hebrews.

2

Jesus, Son of God

Hebrews 1:1 — 2:4

He has spoken to us by a Son.
HEBREWS 1:2

In no sentence of the New Testament are the thoughts so grand and so exquisitely stated as in the opening lines of Hebrews. Verses 1–4 form one majestic sentence in Greek: "God having spoken . . . spoke to us in a Son . . . having cleansed our sins . . . having become . . . far superior to the angels." (Open your Bible. Read the sentence and the chapter out loud. Remember that much of ancient literature was written to be read aloud and to be *heard*.) The wording seems purposefully elaborate. It is as though the marvel of God's speaking through Jesus could only be expressed in the most exalted language possible.

Overture (1:1 — 4)

Verses 1–4 may be described as the prologue or overture. In a dramatic musical production the orchestra first
plays the overture, which introduces some of the main
themes of the program. The author's opening verses function in the same way and summarize the basic message
of Hebrews. God's full and decisive revelation is given in
Jesus Christ. The author does not introduce himself as the
writer but God as the speaker and the Son as the Glorious One through whom the word is spoken. The strong
implication is that we should take heed.

It is not that God has never spoken. The same God who
has spoken through Christ spoke in various ways to the
Jewish fathers through the prophets. But what a contrast
between prophets and Son! The prophets, though God's
inspired men, at their highest were only men. Jesus is far
different. The description of him here is strangely unique.
Although many English translations obscure it, the author
literally says that God has spoken "in Son." "By a Son"
conveys the thought well—he has the rank and dignity of
a Son (cf. 3:6; 5:8; 7:28). He is not just a spokesman, he is
Son. And precisely because he is Son, there is much difference between the ancient "fathers" and our own situation. Besides, God has spoken to us climactically, literally,
"at the end of the days." These are the days ushered in with
Christ's coming, destined to last until he appears "a second time" (9:28).

How shall the author describe God's Son? Writing to
readers who depreciated him, he points out seven things
about the Son.

1. He has been appointed heir of everything.
2. He is the one through whom God made the universe.
3. He radiates the glory of God.

4. He is the perfect likeness of God's being.
5. He sustains the universe with his powerful word.
6. He made cleansing for sins.
7. He took his seat at the right hand of God.

In all things, the Son holds the place of undisputed pre-eminence. He is above all.

1. The Son is heir. Why is this first in the list? In Hebrew thought, there is a vital connection between sonship and heirship, especially if one is the only or unique son. Perhaps the author is already thinking of Psalm 2, which he quotes in verse 5 and applies to Jesus. Psalm 2:8 speaks of the nations and the ends of the earth as the son's "heritage." The Son shares ownership of all things with God the Father. Further, the idea of heirship ("heirs," "inherit," etc.) is important in Hebrews and especially for us, for we are the heirs of salvation (1:14; cf. 6:17).

2. The Son is Creator. Through the agency of the Son the whole universe of space and time came into existence. "Through him all things were made; without him nothing was made" (John 1:3 NIV). "There is . . . one Lord, Jesus Christ, through whom are all things and through whom we exist" (1 Cor. 8:6; cf. Col. 1:16). Of course, only God is Creator, and the author wishes to underscore all the way through that the Son is God as much as God the Father is God.

3. The Son is the brightness of God's glory. If, as John states, no one has ever seen God (John 1:18), then no one has ever seen the glory of God. So Jesus came as the Real Light into the world (John 1:9), and John says, "we saw his glory," glory such as an only Son has (John 1:14). In Jesus the disciples saw the outshining of God's brilliant glory. There was a time when God was without a world, but there never was a time when God was without glory.

4. The Son is the exact representation of God's nature. The Greek word, found only here in the New Testament,

is *charakter*, which means a "stamp" or "impression." The Son is the *character* of God, as a perfect facsimile reproduces the original. Anyone who sees and hears the Son sees and hears God (cf. John 14:9; Col. 1:15). In the Son dwell all the qualities that make God be God.

5. The Son is the sustainer of the universe. He not only is Creator, but he is ruler of the cosmos. He leads and directs and guides it in the way he wants it to go. He has the whole universe in his hand! And he rules the universe, the author says, by his powerful word. In the beginning the word of God spoke worlds into existence; now the word of the Son controls these worlds. Clearly, such ideas suggest again the Godness of the Son.

6. The Son is the redeemer from sin. The long sentence on the Son is building to a climax. What the Son is and does is very important, but the author wants to stress in this letter what the Son has achieved with reference to sin. He made "purification for sins." The Son can be Creator and heir and sustainer, and remain in heaven. However, in order for him to deal adequately with sin, he had to come to earth and become man. This very thing he did. Christ's offering of himself is a special theme in Hebrews, and here we have a clue to its significance.

7. The Son sat down at the Father's right hand. The words denote both triumph and completion. Having purged our sins, he took his seat royally at God's hand. The sitting itself suggests that there was nothing more to be done (cf. 10:11–12). "The right hand," of course, is the place of distinction and honor. Although he was humiliated on earth (12:2–3), he was enthroned in heaven.

With his listing of the seven characteristics of the Son, the author is now able to conclude his grand sentence. He states that the Son has been made "as much superior to angels as the name he has obtained [inherited NRSV] is more excellent than theirs" (v. 4). "Name" may well refer to Christ's dignity and rank, but in view of the next verse (v. 5), "name" probably refers to "Son." No angel was ever called "Son." The word "superior" or "better" is a key word, and we will want to take note of it all through our study.

Christ is superior to the angels. Why talk about this? Are there not other topics that are more interesting to consider? Many people today may think so, but in recent years there actually has been an increasing interest in angels. Certainly, angels are in Scripture and play a significant role as special servants of God. If angels were important for the first readers of Hebrews, should they not be for us today? Is there not a higher, unseen, spirit order of beings, both good and bad? A Christian believes in the unseen things and bases his/her life on the reality of these things.

Christ above the angels is a major concern for the author. Perhaps some of his readers were given to the worship of angels (cf. Col. 2:18). Perhaps some, if they were tempted to fall back into Judaism, were willing to confess Jesus as an angel and avoid the stumbling block of Jesus as God. Or perhaps, since the law of Moses was given through the angels (Acts 7:53; Gal. 3:19), the author wished to establish from the outset that just as Christ is over the angels, his covenant and ministry are superior to any Jewish rival. Whatever the explanation, the Son above the angels becomes the author's subject matter for the rest of chapter 1 and most of chapter 2.

The Son Higher than the Angels (1:5—14)

Earlier we saw how the framework of Hebrews is built on selected Old Testament passages. Such a framework shows not only the importance of the Old Testament but also how much its history and promises find their ultimate meaning in Christ. Following his seven characteristics of the Son, the author cites seven quotations from the Old Testament. He has affirmed the divinity of the

Son; now he proves it. He introduces several of his quotations simply by "he says," meaning, "God says." The author views the Scriptures as the voice of God.

One thing more needs to be added. It is not true that the author quotes his texts out of context and makes them mean something they never meant. Indeed, the opposite is true. He takes, for example, a quotation that originally applied to a Davidic king or prince. (Often his quotations are from one of the "royal" psalms, so called because they concern an Old Testament king.) If it can be said poetically of some Davidic king, "You love righteousness and hate wickedness" (Ps. 45:7), it literally and truthfully can be said that the Son (also a Davidic king) gives these words their full meaning. If it is said that God "in the beginning . . . laid the foundations of the earth" (Ps. 102:25 NIV), the same language also applies to the Son because he, too, is God and Creator. The author's method is neither to wrench passages out of their original contexts nor to apply them haphazardly. Certainly every Old Testament passage has its own setting and time, but God's Spirit through the prophets foresaw in these passages a more complete fulfillment in Christ.

Having stated that the Son is infinitely superior to the angels (1:4), the author proceeds to prove this from the Scriptures. He quotes seven passages from the Old Testament, which to him are incontrovertibly true. These passages, along with his discussion of them, fill up the remainder of chapter 1. The seven passages are employed, on one hand, to demonstrate the absolute divinity of the Son, and, on the other, to show that angels and Son are of different categories and that the Son far excels all angels. Now let's get a bird's-eye view of these quotations and see how they fit the author's arguments concerning the Son.

1. He is the Father's Son (1:5). The first quotation is from Psalm 2:7, a significant line from a royal psalm. At what time did God call Gabriel or Michael in and say, "You are

my Son. Today I have begotten you"? Angels as a group may be referred to as "sons of God" (Job 1:6; 2:1), but no individual angel has ever been called "son of God." Although the original setting for Psalm 2 may refer to the enthronement of David, the author recognizes its fuller meaning to be only in the Messiah (cf. Acts 13:33).

The second quotation is from 2 Samuel 7:14. When did God ever say to an angel, "I will be his Father, and he will be my Son"? (NIV). Originally, the words were spoken of Solomon, David's son. But the author knows that in Solomon these words never found their fullest sense. David had a greater Son than Solomon (cf. Matt. 12:42), and his connection with his Father fulfilled the ideal Father and Son relationship. Of course, no angel ever had such a relationship with the Father.

2. He is the firstborn who is worthy of worship (1:6–7). The third quotation is introduced by speaking of Christ as "firstborn" (NIV), which is an echo of another royal psalm (see Ps. 89:19–29, esp. 27). "Firstborn" does not mean "born first," for David who is called "firstborn" (Ps. 89:27) was not the first son to be born in his family (see 1 Sam. 16:6–13). The term denotes superior rank and is so used elsewhere of Jesus (Rom. 8:29; Col. 1:15, 18; Rev. 1:5).

The quotation, "Let all God's angels worship him," is from the Septuagint (Deut. 32:43; Ps. 97:7). The Septuagint is a Greek translation of the Old Testament, which the author naturally would use. Perhaps the author has in mind the birth of Jesus, or perhaps, his ascension and reintroduction to the heavenly hosts. The author's point is that God commands all the angels to worship the Son. This is still another way of saying that the Son is God, for only God is to receive worship.

The fourth quotation lends support to the contrast of angels and Son. Angels are servants, like "winds" and "flames of fire." They respond when God beckons. They do not command; they obey. The quotation again is from the Septuagint (Ps. 104:4).

3. He is God enthroned and the Anointed One (1:8–9). The fifth quotation is from another royal psalm (Ps. 45) used at a royal wedding. The first part describes a Davidic monarch and the nature of his reign. The author sees that the ultimate fulfillment of the language is the Messiah, the Anointed One, who "loved righteousness" and whose kingdom lasts "for ever and ever." Notice in the quotation that the Son is called "God" and that God the Father is said to be his "God."

4. He is Eternal Creator (1:10–12). The sixth quotation, from Psalm 102:25–27, describes God as Creator. He as Lord "in the beginning . . . laid the foundations of the earth" (NIV)—a beautiful word-painting of creation. But the words equally apply to the Son, for he is Creator (cf. 1:2). One day he will roll the heavens up and toss them aside like an old garment. All things will disintegrate, but "Jesus Christ is the same yesterday and today and forever" (13:8).

5. He is King (1:13–14). The seventh quotation is again from one of the royal psalms (Ps. 110) and concludes the argument in chapter 1. No angel has ever been told, "Sit at my right hand until I make your enemies a footstool" (NIV). No angel sits in God's presence, certainly not at his right hand. But the Son sits royally until every last foe is put under him. Angels serve. They are sent messengers. Why? They serve "those who will inherit salvation" (NIV). That is, they serve for their sake (see 1:14 in RSV, NRSV). Their ministry focuses on the salvation of mankind.

A Great Salvation (2:1 – 4)

The very last word in chapter 1 is "salvation" and this is the leading idea in the opening verses of chapter 2. Verses 2:1–4 form a parenthesis in which the author pauses to exhort his readers. Remember, this is characteristic of the author.

Having established the Son's divinity and his unrivaled supremacy over the angels, he urges that "we must pay more careful attention . . . to what we have heard" (NIV). What have we heard?

Simply, the grandest message ever presented to man, the gospel, the good news of salvation centered in Jesus Christ. And we must give extreme care in heeding it. Practically, it means that when we go to church, we should be anxiously sitting on the edge of the pews to hear God's word preached. If we do not, we may "drift away." Notice: the antidote for drifting is paying attention to what God has said.

The author mentions again the "angels," this time in connection with their message. The law of Moses was transmitted through the angels (Acts 7:53; cf. Gal. 3:19), and no violation of that law was allowed to go unpunished. It imposed penalties on everyone who transgressed it. If angels could not be disobeyed, what will be the consequence of ignoring the Son?

The author's argument is compelling and especially striking for Christian readers. Laying stress to his original word structure, the author is asking, "How shall *we* escape if we neglect such a great *salvation?*" "We" and "salvation" are the words that stand out. We, Christians, have an advantageous position, with consequent obligations. Our status likewise is pronounced, for to us belongs "such a great salvation."

The author proceeds to describe this salvation. It is great because it has a threefold authentication. (1) "It was declared at first by the Lord." The earlier message was spoken by angels, the later by the Lord himself. (2) It "was confirmed to us by those who heard him" (NIV). Although neither readers nor author were ear or eye witnesses of Christ, others, such as the apostles, actually heard him and authenticated his teachings. (3) "God also testified to it by signs and wonders and various miracles and gifts of the Holy Spirit" (NIV). God, through various supernatural works, provided full confirmation of the apostolic witness to Christ.

So the author brings to an end his urgent exhortation. The first readers of Hebrews had certainly heard the good news of salvation. Their excuse could not be that they had never heard. Nor can we absolve ourselves so easily. Those who received just punishment in the Mosaic period are a warning to the original readers and to us. The gospel brings greater privileges and greater responsibilities. Shall we presume on God's grace?

All through the opening section of his letter, the author has been confronting his readers with a choice. First, they must decide about Jesus. Is he or is he not the Son of God? The author has presented him as divine and as one loftier than all the angels. But the readers themselves must answer the fundamental question about Jesus. Second, they must decide about Jesus' message. Are they going to drift away from his saving words, or are they going to anchor their lives in him?

The author pleads with them, and with us, to accept God's final message through his Son. What more can God say? God has sent his "beloved son" (read Mark 12:1–9). What more can God do? There is no alternative but judgment. "How shall we escape if we neglect such a great salvation?" And "such a great salvation" has been offered by the Lord Jesus.

Beautiful Savior! . . . Son of God . . .

QUESTIONS

1. Why are the opening lines of Hebrews all-important? How do they suggest the theme of the letter?
2. List the seven descriptions of Christ as God's Son. Which of these is especially developed throughout the letter?
3. Much of chapters 1 and 2 discuss Christ and the angels. Why was this important to the readers? Is it important for us today?
4. Read Psalm 110. How is this psalm used in chapter 1? How is it used in other parts of Hebrews? (You may want to use a concordance.)
5. Read Psalm 45 and Psalm 102. What are their original settings? How do they find their ultimate fulfillment in Christ?
6. Hebrews 2:1–4 is the first exhortation directly addressed to the readers. What is the substance of this exhortation? What is the key word in the exhortation?

3

Jesus, Son of Man

Hebrews 2:5—18

He had to be made like his brothers.
HEBREWS 2:17 NIV

Hebrews 1 is a majestic chapter on Jesus the Son of God. The author has a wonderful way of announcing to his readers the main themes or subjects he wants to consider. In 1:4 he states his theme for the first two chapters—CHRIST, SUPERIOR TO THE ANGELS. In chapter 1, he contrasts Jesus as Son of God with the angels. In chapter 2, he continues to contrast Jesus with the angels, but now along the lines of Jesus as son of man. For a short time he became a human being, for a little while he was made lower than the angels. Why? The answer to this question becomes the chief topic of chapter 2.

Our previous study concluded with a short exhortation section (2:1–4). All of us need exhortation, and as we go through Hebrews, we must prepare ourselves to respond to the author's exhortations. "How in the world," he asks, "can we escape if we neglect such a great salvation that was brought by the Lord?" "Neglect" contrasts with "paying attention to" in 2:1 and anticipates the author's later discussion of apostasy. What a tragedy that the readers might not realize the greatness of their salvation and turn their backs on the gospel!

The Son's Humiliation and Glory (2:5–9)

With verse 5 the author resumes his discussion of Christ and the angels (1:5–14). Since 2:1–4 is a kind of parenthesis, we need to go from 1:14 to 2:5 in order to grasp the sequence of thought. Angels serve (1:14), and now the author adds an additional point: it was not to angels that God subjected the "world to come" (2:5). "World to come" (cf. "age to come," 6:5) is to be understood from an Old Testament point of view, when people looked forward to "the coming age," that is, "the days of the Messiah." God did not subject the Messianic world order to angels, but to the Son.

Citation of Scripture is enough to prove the point. The Scripture quoted is Psalm 8:4–6. Psalm 8 is a psalm of creation, which contrasts the glory of God the Creator with the glory of man the creature. The psalmist looks at the night sky, the moon and the stars, the work of God's fingers, and marvels at mankind's insignificance—"What is man?"

Yet the psalmist finds that the answer to his question has already been given in Genesis (see Gen. 1:26–30).

There man (mankind) was given dominion over creation, all sheep, oxen, birds, and fish. In terms of this dominion men and women were made in the image of God. The psalmist wonderfully recalls this and reaffirms man's honorable position—he was made just a little below the angels. (The Hebrew word *elohim* can be translated either "angels" or "God.") At creation God crowned man with "glory and honor."

At creation, too, everything was put under man. That was the way it was in the beginning; that was God's original plan. But something has gone awry. Sin has made its ugly entrance into the world. Weakness and disease and death are in evidence all around. Mankind always seems to be fighting a futile battle. Not much of man's original glory is left. At present we do not see everything put under man.

But, the author goes on to say, "We see Jesus . . . crowned with glory and honor" (v. 9). The statement is significant, and the verse is a key verse. It marvelously leads the way for the rest of the chapter (2:10–18) and dramatically asserts several things to be true in Jesus.

1. Jesus is the realization and the true fulfillment of Psalm 8. This, of course, is the point of the contrast in verses 8 and 9. We do not see, not yet at least, everything under man's control. But what do we see? We see Jesus at God's right hand (1:13) with everything under or soon to be under him; and if he is at God's side, he is certainly "crowned with glory and honor." The words of the psalm, then, have their meaning in Christ.

2. "Jesus" is now the name employed by the author. Previously, he has spoken of him as "Son" and "Lord." But in this verse, the author for the first time uses the human name "Jesus" and this in connection with his suffering for humanity.

3. Jesus' position on earth, as man's was in the beginning, was that of one who was made "a little lower than

the angels." The expression "a little" can also be translated "a little while," and the latter may be the author's precise thought. Yes, the Son had to become man, but his earthly humiliation was only for a short while. Now he is crowned with glory and honor.

4. Jesus is crowned with honor *because* he suffered death. Here for the first time the author refers to Jesus' death, and he purposely describes it as "suffering." The idea of suffering is prominent in Hebrews. Its original readers had already suffered persecution (10:32–34), and persecution still lay ahead of them in the future (12:4–11). Surely they might ask, why does God expect us to suffer? The author's answer is that suffering is the way to glory. Jesus was crowned with glory not in spite of his suffering but because of his suffering. So, readers, take courage. The cross was not a mistake. The Son had to suffer. Christians then, and now, need to be reminded that the God who gives the glory is the God who allows the suffering.

5. Jesus was made "lower than the angels" for a specific purpose. By God's amazing grace, he tasted death for everyone. "Taste death" is a Semitic expression (cf. Mark 9:1; John 8:52), comparing the bitterness of death to something unpleasant to the taste. Jesus experienced death in all its bitterness, death on a cross. So Messiah's death is something not to be ashamed of but to be gloried in.

The Savior of Mankind (2:10–18)

With this section the author concludes his discussion of Christ and the angels. This is not apparent at first, but on reading verse 16 we come again to the subject of the angels. Christ did not assume the nature of angels. To save them, presumably, he could have stayed in heaven. But that is the very point of the author. In order to be the

Savior of mankind, the Son had to become like the sons and suffer like them.

Suppose we read verses 10–18 as one paragraph. What is the main thought? Notice that one word stands out at the beginning and at the end. It is the word "suffer." The Son *had* to suffer. Remember that the author was addressing first-century Christians who realistically were facing persecution and "fear of death" (v. 15). They needed to understand not only why the Messiah had to suffer, but that he, too, was tempted in his suffering and so could extend a helping hand to those who suffer.

Verse 10 states right off that this idea of suffering was "fitting." That is, in God's wisdom it was appropriate that the Son suffer. God, through whom all exists, created man for glory. Man made to be lord became a slave. Yet the beautiful thought here is that God still intends to bring "many sons to glory." "Sons," of course, is generic and refers to all of God's children (v. 14). In order to bring about "their salvation," the Son in God's plan is central. Again, the author extols the Son and his achievements. What is said in the rest of the chapter about the Son can be summed up in five points.

1. *The pioneer* (v. 10). The term itself is of unusual interest and is applied elsewhere to Jesus (cf. Acts 3:15; 5:31; Heb. 12:2). It has a broad range of meanings, but here it seems to denote a pioneer who blazes the trail or opens a path for others to follow. The term is likewise used for a military commander ("captain" KJV). The Greco-Roman world was quite familiar with the concept of a mighty god, such as Hercules, who came to earth to conquer the enemies of mankind. By contrast, not mythologically but in real history, Christ came to open up a new path for man to glory.

Now the author says something astonishing about the Son. He had to be "made perfect" through suffering. What can this mean? Did the Son of God lack perfection? In the moral sense, he lacked nothing, as is stated later (4:15; 7:26). Then what does the perfecting of Jesus refer to?

The answer must be supplied by the context. The very next statement (v. 11) speaks of one who "sanctifies" or "makes holy." This is special priestly language, and the author indeed goes on to speak of Jesus as "high priest in service to God" (v. 17). The Greek translation of the Old Testament, the Septuagint (LXX), often uses the verb "perfect" in the sense of "consecrate" or "ordain" a priest to his office (Exod. 29:9, 29, 33, 35; Lev. 21:10). So the full thought of verse 10 is that God, in bringing men/women to the goal for which they had been created, decided to "perfectly qualify" Jesus as high priest by means of suffering (see 5:9; cf. 7:28). Apart from suffering he lacked the necessary priestly credentials.

2. *The sanctifier* (v. 11). The term "sanctify" is a priestly term. It does not mean simply "set apart," it means "set apart as especially belonging to God." Practically, it means to "holify" or "make holy." Holiness is the necessary condition for entering into the presence of God (see Num. 16:5). In verse 11 the sanctifier is Christ and the sanctified are Christians. Christ, therefore, by his sacrifice has cleansed us from all defilement. From now on in Hebrews, when we read of Christ's sanctifying us, it will always be joined with the offering of his body or his blood (9:13–14; 10:10, 14, 29; 13:12).

3. *The brother* (vv. 11–13). The author completes his thought by saying that sanctifier and sanctified are "all of one." "Of one origin" (RSV), "of the same family" (NIV), "have one Father" (NRSV), illustrate how translations have tried to clear up the author's meaning. Since verse 10 refers to God, "of one" probably indicates God the Father. This is why Christ is not ashamed (cf. 11:16) to call us "brothers" (generic). The Son of God is not ashamed of us? That's true, even though numberless times we feel ashamed of ourselves! But this is not precisely the author's thought.

Rather, he is thinking of Jesus as son of man, a fleshly human being, who does not hesitate to identify himself with the people he saves.

Three quotations from the Old Testament show that Jesus delights to call us his brothers. In all three Jesus is the speaker, clearly suggesting that both author and readers understood these passages as Messianic. The first quotation is from Psalm 22. The opening lines of the psalm are applied by Jesus to himself on the cross—"My God, my God, why hast thou forsaken me?" (Matt. 27:46; Mark 15:34). But the dejected tone of the psalm's opening is transformed into joyful thanksgiving. "I will tell of thy name to my brothers; in the midst of the congregation I will praise thee" (Ps. 22:22). Jesus joins in with his "brothers" and praises God in the "congregation."

The second and third quotations are from Isaiah 8:17 (LXX) and 18. Jesus is represented as saying, "I will put my trust in him," and "Here am I, and the children God has given me." Originally, the prophet Isaiah affirmed his faith in God and saw his own children as "signs" in Israel given by God. But the author sees these words have their full meaning in the Messiah. "I, even I, the Messiah, trust him"—just as everyone else must do. And, "Look at the children God has given me"—thus associating himself with the human family.

4. *The liberator* (vv. 14–16). Picking up the word "children" in the previous verse (v. 13), the author declares the reality of the incarnation. Because the "children" are flesh and blood, Jesus, too, partook of the same human nature (literally, "the same things," NRSV). Jesus became man in order to destroy the power of the devil (cf. 1 John 3:8). We should notice that, according to Biblical writers, the devil is real and is here described as the one who "holds the power of death." That is, he *did*. But Jesus came to "destroy" his power, to nullify it and render it ineffec-

tive. In this sense, once and for all, he "abolished death" (2 Tim. 1:10).

Jesus, then, is the one who has the "keys of death and Hades." "I was dead," he says, "and, behold, I am alive for ever and ever" (Rev. 1:18 NIV). So completely did he identify himself with humanity, he died. As Son of God he could have come down from the cross, as son of man he had to stay on the cross. The purpose of his incarnation, the author says, was that "through death" he might overthrow Satan "and set free" all those who throughout their lives were slaves to the "fear of death."

The picture in these verses is a picture of Jesus as conqueror and liberator. In ancient times it was customary for nations at war to appoint champions to represent them in battle. In the Old Testament, it is the Lord God who is champion of his people, who "goes forth like a mighty man, like a man of war . . . against his foes" (Isa. 42:13; cf. Isa. 49:24–26). Likewise, in the New Testament, it is Jesus who "by the finger of God" casts out demons and enters the strong man's house and resoundingly defeats Satan (Luke 11:20–22). So, also, in Hebrews, Jesus is champion of his people. Men and women lived their lives in fear of death, as though captives in a grim prison. But Jesus appeared as a victorious captain or leader (cf. v. 10), beat back the enemy, flung the prison doors open, and freed the captives.

All along the author has had in mind the distinct contrast of Christ and the angels. Verse 16 refers again to the angels by way of emphasis. It was *not* angels that Christ came to help. No, he came to save "the descendants of Abraham." If taken literally, this would mean that Jesus as a Jew came to help the Jews. But in the next verse (v. 17), the author says that it was necessary for Jesus to be made like his brothers. In context, this does not mean like the Jewish race, but that he was made like the "children," of "flesh and blood" like them (v. 14). Besides, Jesus taught that the true descendants of Abraham are those who do what Abraham did (John 8:39), pointing in effect to Abraham's children of faith (Gal. 3:7, 9, 29).

5. *The high priest* (vv. 17–18). We have already seen (v. 10) that Jesus had to pass through suffering in order to be made "perfect," and that this means Jesus was fully or perfectly qualified to be our priest. But at that point he is not called high priest. The author has a remarkable way of dropping hints here and there, especially of his great themes. And now he conveys another announcement theme; for the first time he states boldly that Jesus has become OUR MERCIFUL AND FAITHFUL HIGH PRIEST. This is a most important subject. Only Hebrews applies the title "high priest" to Jesus, and only in Hebrews is this subject developed at length. In fact, it is the subject which predominates in the large middle section of Hebrews.

If it is the duty of a priest to represent men to God (cf. 5:1), in order to carry out this duty Christ had to be made one with those whom he represents. When the author speaks of Jesus' performing his priestly service to God, he is thinking of the great Day of Atonement. He postpones his description of this until chapters 9 and 10, where with delicate strokes, he portrays Jesus as high priest who makes "atonement for the sins of the people."

The chapter concludes with a further reference to the suffering of Jesus. Keep in mind that the word "suffer" is the key word all through this section; and if it is appropriate to call this section "Jesus, Son of Man," it is because he had to suffer. He suffered and so was tempted. "Because he himself suffered when he was tempted" (NIV) misses the point. The opposite is the case. He was tempted when he suffered, or, "he himself was tested by what he suffered" (NRSV).

Although Jesus was tempted in all kinds of ways, the author is speaking here of his "suffering of death" (v. 9). In death, and all that went with it, he was tempted in particular (5:7–10). This is why "he is able to help those who are tempted" (v. 18). What assurance and comfort these words give, first to those originally addressed who were being severely tested by their sufferings and then to all of us. His was the agony of Gethsemane and the cruelties of a depraved age. And his was the temptation to duck out the back way and escape the cross. Nevertheless, he endured. He, then, is able to help us. Angels serve us (1:14), but they cannot take hold of us and steady us when temptation comes.

So chapter 2 ends on a note of encouragement. Remember, this is the author's practical aim as he writes his "word of exhortation" (13:22). Chapters 1 and 2 well illustrate this. The main theme of these chapters is CHRIST, SUPERIOR TO THE ANGELS (1:4). But the author's treatment of the theme is not dispassionate, nor is the theme itself removed light-years from the readers. If Jesus is something less than the real Son of God, the author cannot conceive of him as the bearer of divine revelation. If he is something less than the real son of man, how can he be the Savior of mankind?

As 1:4 suggests the theme of chapters 1 and 2, the theme of chapters 3, 4, and 5 is announced in 2:17: CHRIST, A MERCIFUL AND FAITHFUL HIGH PRIEST. It will be interesting to see how the author develops this theme. In the meantime, he has already laid the foundation for such a discussion. Jesus proved himself FAITHFUL to God by his never-swerving obedience in his vocation of suffering. Jesus showed himself MERCIFUL by his being made one with ordinary human beings.

The author has posed some all-absorbing questions. Who is the Son? The one who far excels the angels. Why is he, not they, crowned with glory and honor? Because he suffered death. But why did he have to die? In order to be thoroughly equipped as our high priest. And why did he have to resemble his human brothers? Because he came to save them, not the angels, and to be their priest.

So Jesus descended to humiliation. He stooped lower than the angels and became man. Praise God!

> Beautiful Savior! . . . Son of God and Son of Man.
> Glory and honor . . . Now and forevermore be Thine.

QUESTIONS

1. Read Psalm 8. How does the author of Hebrews make use of this psalm?
2. Hebrews 2:9 is a key verse. Can you explain it phrase by phrase?
3. Hebrews 2:9–10 and 18 use the word "suffer." Why is this a significant term for the readers? How was Christ made "perfect through suffering" (v. 10)?
4. Discuss Jesus as "Sanctifier." Why is this an important concept?
5. Discuss Jesus as "Brother." Why was it necessary that Jesus be made like his brothers (v. 17)?
6. Hebrews 2:17 is another key verse. How does the last part of the verse anticipate chapters ahead?

4

Jesus, the Faithful High Priest

Hebrews 3:1 — 4:13

. . . that he might become a . . . faithful high priest.

With easy-to-remember titles, the opening chapters of Hebrews can be outlined as follows:

Chapter 1: Christ, higher than the angels
Chapter 2: Christ, lower than the angels

Or, the titles can be set another way:

Chapter 1: Jesus, Son of God
Chapter 2: Jesus, Son of Man

Although holding a rank far superior to the angels, for a little while he had to be made lower than the angels. Not ceasing to be God, he became man. As man he experienced the frustrations and limitations of flesh. As man he put his trust in God. As man he faced temptation, especially the rigorous temptations of his suffering and death.

The Book of Hebrews especially stresses the real humanity of Jesus. Is there some reason for this? Again and again the author, when referring to Christ, uses the human name "Jesus." Why is this the case? Of course, the human name points to the human Jesus, and, likewise, the human Jesus identifies him with us. But there is more. It is the distinct contribution and recurring affirmation of Hebrews—mentioned nowhere else in the New Testament—that Jesus Christ is our high priest. For the first time this is stated explicitly at 2:17: Jesus was made like his "brothers," that he might be A MERCIFUL AND FAITHFUL HIGH PRIEST (2:17).

These words are placed in caps because this is the theme for the next three chapters. You will recall that the author characteristically announces the subjects he plans to consider. In 1:4 he declares that Christ is superior to the angels, and he develops this theme down through chapter 2. In 2:17 he states that Christ is a merciful and faithful high priest, and then he deals with this topic through 5:10. In doing so he reverses the order, first showing that Christ is a faithful high priest (3:1–4:13) and then presenting Christ as a merciful high priest (4:14–5:10). In other words, the author of Hebrews calls our attention to the *fact* of Jesus' priesthood and then to the inward *qualities* that make his priesthood great.

Jesus and Moses (3:1 — 6)

In chapter 3 the author speaks again to his readers. "Therefore, holy brothers, who share in a heavenly call,

consider Jesus . . . faithful . . ." (vv. 1–2). The thought is
not simply "consider Jesus," but "consider that Jesus was
faithful." Notice that "faithful" in 3:2 clearly connects
with and repeats "faithful" in 2:17. Notice also that the
same word "faithful" is echoed all through these verses—
"faithful" (3:2, 5), "faith" (4:2), "believed" (4:3), "unbelief" (3:12, 19), "disobey" (or "disbelieve," 3:18), and
"disobedience" (or "disbelief," 4:6, 11). The author
clearly wanted to urge his readers to the same "faithfulness" that marked Jesus as "faithful" to God.

The terms of the author's appeal remind the readers of
their high position. They are "holy brothers," made "holy"
by Christ as sanctifier and "brothers" because he identifies himself as one of them. They share in a "heavenly
call," just as they "share" in Christ (3:14) and in the Holy
Spirit (6:4). Their call is from God, a call to heaven itself,
to be expounded further in the heavenly rest for God's
people (Hebrews 4). Plainly, the language is language of
salvation written not to the unsaved but to Christians.

Jesus described as "apostle and high priest" looks
ahead. The terms introduce us to two contrasts that are
to follow, between Christ and Moses and between Christ
and Aaron. The word "apostle" is not merely "one sent"
but denotes "one sent with full authority to carry out his
mission." This applies first and foremost to Christ and
then to his chosen men. Jesus is "high priest" primarily
because he is the one who makes atonement for the sins
of the people (cf. 2:17). The Jewish high priest made his
offering on the Day of Atonement, whose significance
with reference to Jesus is postponed until the climactic
chapter 9. As "apostle" Jesus represents God to man (cf.
1:2), as "high priest" he represents man to God. And he
is high priest of "our confession." "Our" is emphatic. That
is, we and no one else—not the Jews, not the Greeks—
have confessed him. We have committed ourselves to
him. He is the center of everything we believe.

How was Jesus faithful? We have already seen in chapter 2 that he was faithful to God in his pathway of suffering. But the author has more to say because he wants to bring Moses into the picture and show how Jesus was faithful in comparison with Moses. In his Old Testament, the author finds two passages that well illustrate his points. The first is a foreshadowing of Christ, for it speaks of a "faithful priest" and his "sure house" (1 Sam. 2:35). The second, the passage specifically quoted, refers to "my servant Moses," who was "faithful in all God's house" (Num. 12:7).

It is difficult to overstate the importance of Moses to people of Jewish background. Remember that Hebrews probably was first directed to readers of this sort who were being pulled back to the religion of their fathers. So the author will speak of Moses and of his faithfulness and then show how the differences between Moses and Christ outweigh the similarities. Although the Moses/Christ argument has already been implied (2:2–3), it awaits its full development in chapters 8 (vv. 5–6) and 12 (vv. 18–29).

Moses truly was faithful, but the glory of Christ outshines the glory of Moses. To what degree? As much as "the builder of a house has more honor than the house" (v. 3). Do you recall the words "honor" and "glory"? We met them in chapter 2. Jesus is now crowned with the "glory" and "honor" that man had at creation (2:8–9). Jesus himself, of course, is Creator (1:2); he is the Builder of the house. But if God is "the builder of all things" (v. 4), this means that Jesus is God. He is God as much as God the Father is God. No wonder that his glory far excels that of Moses.

Christ is beyond Moses in other respects. Moses was faithful *in* God's house; Christ was faithful *over* God's house (vv. 5–6). And Moses is described as a "servant." No, he is not a "slave." He is not to be disparaged. Moses was an "honored servant" (*therapon*). The term suggests approval and dignity. In particular Moses was a servant

"testifying to what would be said in the future" (NIV).
Here the passive voice is used, which in Scripture often
indicates divine agency. The meaning is that Moses bore
witness to what God in the future was to speak in his Son
(1:2; 2:3).

It was an honor for Moses to be God's servant, but
Christ is exalted as God's Son. He is Son "over God's
house," just as it will be said later that he is a priest "over
the house of God" (10:21). "And we are [God's] house,"
the author adds assuredly. There are not two houses but
one—Moses "in" and Christ "over," yet still only one
house. Christians, not Moses and the Israelites, are God's
people. But there is a condition. The author does not say
that we are God's house, period. We are his house "if"—
if we hold on to "our confidence and hope" (v. 6). Notice
that the "if" is repeated in verse 14. "Confidence" and
"hope" are key terms in Hebrews, where all the way
through so much depends on perseverance. Hope is not
just a wish, not just an inward feeling quietly treasured.
It is active, certain, triumphant. Believers can rejoice in
their hope (cf. Rom. 5:2) because it rests on the achieve-
ment of Christ, so exquisitely pictured in Hebrews.

A Warning from the Past (3:7—19)

We have seen that the author from time to time inter-
rupts his train of thought and admonishes his readers.
With a slight or a lengthier pause, he encourages and
warns. This is now his second pause. In 2:1–4 we have
an exhortation against drifting from God's word, and in
3:7–4:16 we have an exhortation against disbelieving
God's word. The warning comes from the past, when
Israel, in its desert wanderings, stubbornly refused to listen to God. Israel, God's people in the past, did not continue in faith; and the same fear of faithlessness runs

through the mind of the author with respect to God's present people.

The warning begins: "Therefore, as the Holy Spirit says . . ." The words preface an Old Testament quotation from Psalm 95:7–11. The author is saying Scripture is inspired by the Holy Spirit, has a relevant message, and demands a present hearing (cf. 10:15). Psalm 95 was especially well known to the readers, since it was frequently used to introduce worship in the synagogue. This psalm consists of two parts; the first part is a call to worship, and the second is a call for obedience. Long ago, when the psalm was written, there was the firm recognition that worship and obedience must go together.

The author's quotation of the psalm begins with the second part: "Today, when you hear his voice, do not harden your hearts." The words are especially meaningful, for in this section they are quoted three times (cf. vv. 7–8, 15; 4:7). "Today" is emphatic. Today God is speaking through a greater someone than Moses, and today God expects us to respond.

The quotation continues and highlights Israel's unchanging condition of a hard heart. With great excitement the people left Egypt under the leadership of Moses (cf. 3:16); and shortly afterward, at Rephidim, they "put the Lord to the proof" (Exod. 17:1–7). Later, at Kadesh, twelve men from the twelve tribes were chosen to go and "spy out the land" of Canaan. They returned with glowing reports of the land, but they did not believe that God would give them victory over its inhabitants. They rebelled and would not take the land. Because they would not go in, they had to face God's judgment that they would never go in.

And, of course, they did not. God was "provoked" with them and "swore" that they would never enter his "rest." "'As I live,' says the LORD, 'what you have said in my hearing I will do to you; your dead bodies shall fall in this wilderness; and of all your number, numbered from twenty years old and upward, . . . not one shall come into the land where I swore that I would make you dwell, except Caleb . . . and Joshua.'" (Num. 14:28–30; read all of chapters 13 and 14). The land, from which they were shut out, was the "rest" God had in mind for them. But God was exasperated with them, as can be seen in the words "wrath" and "swore" and "provoked." God took an oath and affirmed his set purpose that they would not enter in. He was "provoked" with their unfaithfulness. The author wants all his readers to know that God can be sorely displeased with his people.

The application of Psalm 95 is now made (v. 12). The author says in effect: "Beware! You, like the Israelites, can have a straying, evil heart. They refused to believe God. This can happen to *any* of you, and so lead you to fall away from the living God." The term for "fall away" is *apostenai*, the root word for "apostasy." "Beware" *(blepete)* suggests the gravity of the situation. Only one other time do we have this in Hebrews: "Beware *[blepete]* that you do not refuse him who is speaking" (12:25, my translation). We should be sure to notice that both times "beware" is used to caution against failure to pay attention to God's voice.

The danger of apostasy is real and especially for the first readers of this letter. The winds and rains of temptation were beating against them. Would their house stand? Only if it was founded on Christ. To forsake Christ and go back to Moses and Judaism meant apostasy from the living God. Apostasy is the ultimate consequence of unbelief. "Unbelief" here is not so much "lack of believing" but "refusal of believing." The God who always lives is ready to punish any such apostasy (cf. 10:26–31).

The crisis of the situation demanded individual action: "Exhort one another every day, as long as it is called 'today.'" "Today" picks up the key word in Psalm 95—"today" while there is still opportunity to hear his voice. The Christian life is lived daily, but it is not to be lived exclusively. Believers are to encourage and strengthen each other, and this especially takes place in the worship assembly (cf. 10:24–25). If the original readers were meeting only on the Lord's Day, only once a week, the admonition here is that they are to meet day by day. "Encouragement" or "exhortation" is a vital concern in Hebrews (6:18; 10:25; 12:5; 13:22).

It is possible, the author goes on to say, that the readers can be "hardened by the deceitfulness of sin." The author often uses such rhetorical expressions. He does not say simply, "hardened by sin," but "hardened by the deceitfulness of sin." That is, we are "deceived by sin and so hardened." Sin leads to a hardened heart, a hardened or stubborn heart to unbelief, and unbelief (refusal to believe) to apostasy.

In verse 6 the author says, "We are [God's] house if . . ." He now says in verse 14, "We share in Christ, if . . ." A parent sometimes speaks to a child and says, "We will do so and so, if . . ."—and the child never seems to hear the "if." All Christians must remember the "if" of their final salvation. God is the great God of grace, and we are saved by his grace. But grace must be received and continued in (cf. 2 Cor. 6:1). Indeed, "we have become Christ's partners" (NEB) and we will share his throne (Rev. 3:21), *if* we hold the confidence we had when we began our Christian journey. That confidence or assurance must be held "firm to the end," until Christ comes or until we depart to be with him.

While the "if" is still on their minds, the author quotes again to the readers the lines of Psalm 95:7–8: "Today, when you hear his voice, do not harden your hearts." Then, with an impressive flourish, the author presses his readers with five rhetorical questions. The questions, contained in verses 16–18, with the overall conclusion in verse 19, can be arranged as follows:

1. Question: "Who were they that *heard* and yet were *rebellious?*"
   Answer: "Was it not all those who left Egypt under the leadership of Moses?"
2. Question: "And with whom was he *provoked forty years?*"
   Answer: "Was it not with those who sinned, whose bodies fell in the wilderness?"
3. Question: "And to whom did he *swear* that *they should never enter* his *rest?*"
   Answer: "[Was it not] to those who were disobedient?"

   Conclusion: "So we see that they were unable to enter because of unbelief."

Notice the words in italics, showing that the questions are expressed in words of Scripture (Ps. 95).

What a somber way to conclude chapter 3! The chapter begins with the faithfulness of Christ and ends with the faithlessness of Israel. Which way will the readers choose? One word, stated both at the beginning of the paragraph (v. 12) and at the end (v. 19), stands out above all others—"unbelief." Did God fail the people of Israel? Did Moses? No! They did not enter their hoped-for destination because they refused to believe.

Rest for the People of God (4:1—10)

Although chapter 4 begins here, there really is no break in thought from the preceding chapter. The key word that ties the chapters together is the word "enter." Notice that it appears in the last verse of chapter 3, in the first verse of chapter 4, and seven more times in the following verses. The author, drawing upon Psalm 95, clearly wants to emphasize to his present readers that God still has a rest which is to be *entered*. Picture in your mind, on one hand, God closing his arms to Israel and excluding them from Canaan and, on the other hand, God opening his arms to his people for rest. There he stands with his arms stretched out as wide as they can reach, showing his rest is still available to all. But what is his rest which we are urged to enter?

The author begins a discussion of this rest in a startling manner. His first word (in the Greek text) is "Let us fear." "Let us fear lest any" be found to fall short of that rest. As before (3:12–13), his concern is for every single person in the congregation. "Yes," he says, "it's entirely possible that we might miss the promised rest." How can that be? "For good news came to us just as to them." In the case of the desert generation, their good news was of a land of rest and plenty. On the other hand, Christians have heard the good news that is best of all, the saving news of Christ. Will we respond in faith?

The author now speaks with assurance, that the divine rest is ours. "We who have believed enter that rest." That is, we are in the process of entering that rest, for the context makes it clear we have not yet gained it. That Israel was forbidden to enter God's rest simply shows that he had reserved it for others. Indeed, God's rest has been ready ever since his works were finished from the time of creation.

In the next verses (4–7) three Old Testament quotations demonstrate that God's rest remains open. The first, from Genesis 2:2, is introduced in a vague manner characteristic of the style of Hebrews (cf. 2:6; 5:6). God's rest was prepared long ago, at the end of creation week. There it is said, "God rested . . . from all his works." The second and third quotations are again from Psalm 95, both of which are restatements of what has been said before. But a further thought is added with the words, "Today, when you hear his voice." The Holy Spirit spoke this through David centuries after the desert experiences. This can only mean that God's rest was still available in the time of David; and if it was available then, the author reasons, it must be available for God's people today.

Earlier, there was a distinct contrast between Moses and Christ (3:1–6); here there is a contrast between Joshua and Christ. The names "Joshua" and "Jesus," which actually are different forms of the same name, facilitate the contrast. Moses led the people out of Egypt, but he could not lead them into Canaan. Joshua led them in, but the rest he secured was earthly and temporary. Jesus, our commander and pioneer, is able to lead us to lasting rest.

The conclusion of it all is now reached. "So then, there remains a sabbath rest for the people of God; for whoever enters God's rest also ceases from his labors as God did from his" (vv. 9–10). The word "sabbath rest" (*sabbatismos)* is fascinating in itself and is found nowhere else in the New Testament. It is a special word for God's special rest. It is even possible to translate it "sabbath keeping." If so, we must understand that it is figurative in nature, for the author has been speaking throughout this section of a rest that must be *entered.* Rest—what an awe-inspiring thought! It is as a farmer who comes in after a hard day, tired and foot-sore. He takes off his dusty shoes and lies down to rest. It is as a traveler who completes his lengthy journey, weary and about to drop. He finally gets home for refreshment and rest. God has his own sabbath rest for his own true people—"that they may rest from their labors, for their deeds follow them!" (Rev. 14:13).

The Word of God (4:11–13)

God's perfect rest awaits his people. But the author, reflecting on the status of his readers, sounds a solemn warning: "Let us strive to enter that rest, that no one fall by the same sort of disobedience." "Strive" suggests zeal and exertion. God has graciously provided his heavenly rest, but individual energy is essential to enter it. We are to make every effort possible lest we fall short as Israel did in the desert. In other words, "Let us try hard to go to heaven!"

The next verse begins with "for," clearly connecting with the previous verse. "For the word of God is living and active." The author is urging his readers as follows: "You see what happened to disobedient Israel. When you read God's written word (especially in Psalm 95), don't think it is meaningless. It is always relevant and always applicable." The author wants to get through their thick heads that Israel's awful tragedy can strike his readers as well.

God's message is also like a "double-edged" sword. It can cut through any substance, even severing "soul and spirit" and "joints and marrow." These expressions are rhetorical and are not to be taken literally. The author is merely adding one term to another to describe the keen edge of God's word. It cuts sharply through one's inmost self and "judges the thoughts and attitudes of the heart" (NIV). Here the message of God is personified, as though it is a person. As we read God's word, it sees right into our hearts. It searches and instructs. It warns and encourages.

> Every hour
> I read you kills a sin
> Or lets a virtue in
> To fight against it.

Such is the nature of God's ever-present word. Such is the nature of the all-knowing God. So the author easily moves from God's word to God himself and says in effect, "Before him no creature is hidden. All things are naked and laid bare to his eyes." The scene now is of God as

Judge. Everything in all creation is ranged before his scrutinizing eye. Before him no disguise is conceivably possible. His judgments are infallible. And he will be our Judge, the one "to whom we must give account" (literally, "to whom is our word").

This imposing paragraph thus concludes with emphasis on one term—"word."

v. 12: "For the *word* of God is living and active."

v. 13: "To whom is our *word*."

Because God's living word has been proclaimed to us, we must give our word, our account, back to the Living God.

The issues are serious. Either we go on (6:1), or we fall back and away (3:12). Either we enter God's rest, or we do not. How unimaginably horrible—just the thought, the possibility—that we might stand before him and hear the dreadful words, "They shall never enter my rest"!

QUESTIONS

1. Hebrews 3:1 presents a number of key terms, some of which are restated in 4:14. What do the following terms mean: "holy brothers," "heavenly call," "apostle," "high priest," and "confession"?
2. Compare/contrast the faithfulness of Christ and the faithfulness of Moses. How is the term "faithful" echoed in succeeding verses?
3. The exhortation beginning at 3:7 is based on Psalm 95. Read Psalm 95. What are the main ideas of the psalm? What application does the author of Hebrews make in 3:12–19?
4. Can we, too, be deceived and hardened by sin? According to what we have already read in Hebrews, what is available for us to deal with sin?

5. What is the good news that came to the Israelites and the good news that has come to us (4:2)?

6. God's rest for his people is a rest that is to be "entered." Trace the word "enter" in these verses (4:1–13). How does 4:9–10 contribute to the picture of God's rest?

7. In context, what is the "word of God" that is living and active (4:12)? What does this mean? How are verses 11, 12, and 13 connected?

5

Jesus, the Merciful High Priest

Hebrews 4:14—5:10

> *. . . that he might become a merciful . . . high priest.*
>
> HEBREWS 2:17

There is a rest that is worth everything; and, paradoxically, we are "to *strive* to enter that *rest*" (4:11). God's own rest for God's own people—prepared by God from the beginning, promised to faithless Israel, unfulfilled by Joshua, accessible in David's time, and still awaiting its complete realization. This is the gist of what the author has been saying as he warns his first readers and us.

And a further warning is in order. God's word is not just something written down long ago in Psalm 95, but it is always living and effective. It is something that sees us as we are. Certainly, when we face God's final judgment, it is sheer folly to think that we can deceive him.

God's demands are great, but his mercy is great as well. It is significant that, immediately after this long warning (3:7–4:13), the author begins to develop the theme of Jesus as the merciful high priest. Verses 14–16, the last verses of chapter 4, serve as a bridge, a transition section from solemn warning to uplifting teaching on the high priesthood of Jesus.

The Compassionate Christ (4:14–16)

We are to remember 2:17 as a very pivotal verse, which declares that Jesus is a merciful and faithful high priest. In 3:1–6 the author treats Jesus as faithful; now he begins to discuss Jesus as merciful.

Verse 14 states several things in particular about our high priest. First, he is our great high priest. Christians surely do have a high priest, although some of the original readers may have had doubts on this point. And he is great! He far excels all his predecessors, as the author will go on to show, in both his character and his work.

Second, our high priest "has passed through the heavens." Again, the language is rhetorical. We have seen that such language is typical of the author, which calls attention here to Jesus' exalted state. We have also seen that the author loves to use language of analogy. The Jewish high priest passed through an earthly veil into the Holy of Holies, but our high priest has gone into the divine presence in heaven (9:24).

Third, our high priest is none other than Jesus, the Son of God. The terms focus on the complementary aspects of his nature, his humanity and his divinity, which set the stage for further discussion (5:1–10) on the merciful high priest.

Since we have Jesus as our great high priest, the author presses his readers by saying, "let us hold fast our confession." As Christians we do have a "confession" (3:1).

We have confessed Christ; we have put our faith and hope in him. Now we are urged to "hold fast" to him and everything we believe in because of him. The implication is that the first readers of Hebrews were wavering in their allegiance to Christ. The same thing, of course, can happen to us.

In the ancient world the general feeling was that the gods were far removed from mortals. The author has already dealt extensively with this and has smashed such notions with reference to the true God. Now, encouragingly, he states that Christ is not aloof from his followers. Negatively expressed: we do not have a high priest who is "unable to sympathize with our weaknesses." Our word "sympathize" is actually a Greek word, found in the New Testament only here and in 10:34. The term, which literally means "feel with," in English often refers to the sharing of grief or pity. That is not the thought here, but rather that Christ, since he also was human, has "fellow-feelings with" weak human beings. Positively expressed: he is "one who in every respect has been tempted as we are, yet without sinning." Temptation in itself is not sinful. Fully human, Jesus knew equally poverty, toothache, and beguiling desire. He was tested "in every respect." But, as is stated elsewhere, he never once yielded to sin (cf. 2 Cor. 5:21; 1 Peter 2:22; 1 John 3:5).

Knowing that our high priest is near, "let us then with confidence draw near to the throne of grace" (v. 16). "Confidence" is the same word as the word for "boldness," even "courage." It is no wonder that the author urges boldness on us. One might think, "Here I am today covered up with self and sin and unkept promises. How can I go to God?" Nevertheless, "take courage," the author says, "draw near boldly." "Draw near" is a technical term used to describe Old Testament priests as they "approached" God in worship. The thought here not only is that the door is open, but through Christ we can come directly before God.

More specifically, the exhortation is to persistent prayer. "Throne of grace" is the author's wonderful way of referring to "the throne of God." Earlier in 4:13, God is represented on a throne of judgment, from whose all-scrutinizing eye no one can escape. Now the author, as he ends chapter 4, intentionally pictures God on a throne of grace. "Grace" and "mercy" and "help" are what we all need, and none of us more than early Christians who were under the daily threat of persecution. And grace is at God's throne, whenever we need it. If this be so, why do we cower and hang back? The author encourages the opposite. The full force of his exhortation is, "Let us again and again draw near in prayer to the throne of grace. Let us draw near to God!"

As we look back over Hebrews 4:1–16, we should keep in mind that the whole chapter presents a marvelous combination of warnings and exhortations. Over the years I have tried to teach my students that there are *four* things to remember about chapter *four.* Expressed in another way, there are 4 "let-us-es" in chapter 4:

1. "Let us fear." (4:1)
2. "Let us . . . strive to enter that rest." (4:11)
3. "Let us hold fast our confession." (4:14)
4. "Let us . . . draw near to the throne of grace." (4:16)

Qualifications of the High Priest (5:1 – 4)

We have now arrived at a further stage of the author's argument on Jesus as high priest. He has affirmed that Christians do indeed have a high priest; that priest is Jesus, and Jesus as priest is both faithful and merciful. But does he fit the priestly requirements set down in the Old Testament?

Generally speaking, the high priest, whether of the old order or of the new, had to meet two qualifications: (1) he must be "selected from among men" (v. 1) and, (2) he must be "called by God" (v. 4). After stating these general qualifications, with additional reflections on them (5:1–4), the author proceeds, in reverse order, to apply them to Christ (5:5–10).

"For every high priest chosen from among men" (v. 1) begins the author's direct discussion on priesthood. The conjunction "for," however, connects back with chapter 4, in particular with the sympathizing high priest (4:13). Taken from his fellowmen, he is their representative before God, offering "gifts and sacrifices for sins." The language used is deliberately vague, allowing the author to focus later on the role of the high priest in dealing with sin on the Day of Atonement (chapters 9 and 10).

As an ordinary man, the high priest was "subject to weakness." This meant, on one hand, that it was necessary for him (Lev. 16:1–24) "to offer sacrifice for his own sins as well as for those of the people" (v. 3). That is, the Jewish high priest was in spiritual distress as much as were the people.

On the other hand, since the high priest as a human was clothed in weakness, "he can deal gently with the ignorant and wayward" (v. 2). At least, this is the way it ought to be. All through here the author is viewing the high priest from an ideal point of view. According to the law of Moses, the high priest was supposed to be a very holy man, one who was arrayed in gorgeous robes, the religious leader of the entire nation. In point of fact, most of the Jewish high priests fell far short of the divine requirement. In Roman times, many were outrageously corrupt, plotting and maneuvering for political favor. Oh, how often the deep-thinking, pious Jew must have lamented the degraded condition of the Jewish high priests! How often he must have lifted eyes and voice to heaven longingly crying out for a new and better and real high priest who could properly represent man to God.

The author knows well that only Jesus meets the conditions of that longed-for high priest. Only he can "deal gently" (v. 2) with those going astray. The word translated "deal gently" is rare in the Greek language. It is a "middle word," standing between the extremes of indifference and sentimental indulgence. For example, some parents don't care about their children at all. Whether they are fed or clothed or out on the streets are matters of little concern to them. Other parents "love" their children so much that they allow them to do almost anything. A child can storm in the house with muddy feet, scatter his room topsy-turvy, and even demolish the furnishings. And the parents only say, "He's just a child. Isn't he cute?"

Now the point is that Jesus, our high priest, deals moderately and gently with us. He does not overindulge us, nor does he turn in indifference away from us. He moderates his anger toward us and bears with our mistakes. He is the supreme ideal of what a high priest ought to be.

What is more: "One does not take the honor [of high priest] upon himself; but he is called by God, just as Aaron was" (v. 4). Aaron, Moses' brother, the first high priest, was called by God (Exod. 28; Lev. 8). This is the first mention of Aaron in Hebrews, by which the author begins to establish an important comparison/contrast between Jesus and Aaron and all his priestly descendants. Anyone who would arrogate priesthood to himself lacks the quality of compassion so essential to the office.

Qualifications of Jesus (5:5—10)

The previously stated requirements of the Old Testament high priest are now carefully applied to Jesus. "So also Christ did not exalt (literally, "glorify") himself to be made a high priest" (v. 5). Notice that "Jesus" (4:14) is now referred to as "Christ." That he is here called "Christ"

fits his divine appointment. In his preexistent state, before
he entered the world, Christ did not cling tenaciously to
his equality with God (Phil. 2:6–8), but willingly came
to earth as a servant. Nor while he was on earth did he
campaign for the office of high priest.

Patiently and submissively, Christ waited for his call
to become high priest. There in Scripture is the record of
his call. God who appointed him declared,

> "Thou art my Son,
> today I have begotten thee." (v. 5)

In another place the call reads,

> "Thou art a priest for ever,
> after the order of Melchizedek." (v. 6)

Together the two passages attest to Christ's sonship and
priesthood, and to his call from God.

It needs to be emphasized that we have here one of the
great contributions of this marvelous letter of Hebrews.
No other book in the New Testament sees so clearly the
inseparable connection of sonship/kingship/messiahship/
priesthood. At ancient Qumran, where it seems many of
the Dead Sea Scrolls were produced, the people expected
two messiahs, only one of whom had priestly credentials.
But the author of Hebrews, and presumably the early
church, recognized that true sonship demanded identity
of messiahship and priesthood.

Hebrews contributes significantly in another respect.
According to the Old Testament, the high priestly office
was strictly hereditary. To be a priest, one had to be of the
tribe of Levi. But to be a high priest, one had to be of a particular family of Levi, physically descended from Aaron.
All Jews knew this. Then how could Jesus who was neither a Levite nor an Aaronite become high priest?

"Look again at Scripture," the author says. "You will remember that we read from Psalm 2, 'Thou art my Son. . . .' Now, turn again. What does Psalm 110 say? 'Thou art a priest for ever, after the order of Melchizedek.' So there it is. The same collection of Psalms that says Christ is God's Son also says that Christ is priest."

The author will expand on all of this later.

In still another respect, Hebrews adds immeasurably to our understanding of Jesus. Verses 7–10 allow us to see Jesus in a way not revealed in any of the Four Gospels, and so these verses remain a treasure for all lovers of Hebrews and lovers of its majestic Christ.

This little unit of verses is also recognized as a literary gem—another of the author's moving, artistically constructed sentences of which he is so fond. The four verses form one sentence in Greek. Lucid, well-thought-out, so rhythmic in form, so exalted in concept, some have argued that the passage is an early Jewish-Christian "hymn of the high priest." But this is an unnecessary hypothesis. It should be remembered that Hebrews in so many other places exhibits the work of a practiced hand, and that this sentence flows smoothly from the master-thoughts of 4:17, 5:2, and 5:5–6.

In 5:5 the author states that Christ did not presume the honor of the high priestly office. To illustrate his point, he casts a backward look at Jesus on earth. "In the days of his flesh, Jesus offered up prayers and supplications, with loud cries and tears" (v. 7). Did you notice that unusual expression, "days of his flesh"? The New Testament has numbers of such expressions because Christ is so absolutely unique. We speak of no one else in such terms, for human beings have never known anything but "days of flesh." But the language is apropos for Christ, with the implication that he had/has other days that are not "fleshly days."

The reference to "prayers and supplications," along with "loud cries and tears," quite clearly alludes to Jesus' prayer in Gethsemane. In that hour of his deep sorrow, he cast himself upon God "who was able to save him from death." In Gethsemane, according to Luke, he knelt in "anguish" (Luke 22:44 NRSV), which literally means "agony." "Agony" is actually a Greek word that has passed into English. It is remarkable that Luke alone uses this word as he describes Jesus' sufferings, and this not in connection with the cross but of his struggles in Gethsemane.

For what did Jesus pray, and what does it mean when it says, "he was heard because of his reverent submission" (v. 7 NRSV)? As Mark expresses it, he said, "Abba, Father . . . take this cup from me; yet not what I will, but what thou wilt" (Mark 14:36). Was this prayer answered? Yes, emphatically! Verse 7 says, "he was heard." How? Notice that the prayer of Jesus included two petitions. The first was for physical deliverance, the second humbly submitted to the wisdom and will of God. The first request was not granted, but the second was because the prayer was prayed with a heart of "reverent submission" that left it all up to God.

The thought of 2:10 is now brought in again, for even sonship does not exclude suffering. "Although he was a Son, he learned obedience through what he suffered" (v. 8). Learning and suffering are linked together in a familiar wordplay facilitated by the similar sound of the two words (*emathen . . . epathen*, "he learned" . . . "he suffered"). Sometimes a person has to learn the hard way. Boldly, the author applies this to Jesus. Son though he was, he had to learn the hard way, as though he was a hardhead. What did he have to learn? Obedience, even to death on a cross (cf. Phil. 2:8), to the furthest point beyond which he could not go.

The author sees all this as indispensable for the Son. "And being made perfect he became the source of eternal salvation to all who obey him" (v. 9). Here we meet again the distinctive vocabulary of Hebrews and its special use of the word "perfect." You may recall that we first saw this in 2:10, which says that Christ was made "perfect through suffering." There and here the idea is that Christ, on the basis of suffering, was "perfectly qualified" to be our high priest. Having successfully gone through the school of suffering, he became the "source" or "cause" of our salvation. And the salvation he achieved is truly "eternal" (cf. 6:2; 9:12, 14, 15; 13:20), held in reserve for "all who obey him." If he unceasingly obeyed as Son, can we do less?

Having begun his paragraph (5:5) by saying that Christ did not glorify himself to be made high priest, the author now concludes the paragraph with the same thought. Christ was the one who was "designated," that is, the one clearly named by God as "a high priest after the order of Melchizedek" (v. 10). This divine announcement of a new order of priesthood can only mean that the old order of Aaronic priests has passed away. The new priestly order, like that of Melchizedek, becomes the subject highlighted in the central portion of Hebrews.

Now let us reflect on this lofty passage and see if there are some practical lessons that we can draw from it. After all, sublime as it may be, this is not just a profound, esoteric piece of theology. It may supply answers, or clues at least, to some of life's most bewildering problems.

1. What does this passage teach us about Christ? Here we come face to face with the magnificent high priest of the Christian religion. He supersedes all previous high priests, especially because he can deal gently with us.

This much we grant and appreciate. But do we begin to comprehend the meaning of his becoming flesh and of his entering Gethsemane? Why did he leave his clinically pure, air-conditioned heaven and come to earth? And why did he undergo so much pain in the garden?

Our modern, quick-answer mentality does not relate to these questions. We never quite seem to grasp how hard it was for Jesus in all the circumstances of his earthly life. Too often we picture him as Son of God only, as though everything was smooth for him, as though he just glided through life with the ease of an ice-skater. Even portraits painted of Jesus in Gethsemane are refined and neat, with every hair of his head in place.

But the author views him differently. He takes a picture of Jesus in his weakest hour. Purposely, he exposes the grim reality of Jesus' sufferings. He points to Gethsemane. If ever there was a time when Jesus was "beset with weakness," it was there. Through such suffering he was made "perfect."

2. What does this passage teach us about prayer? It expressly teaches that not every request we make in prayer will be granted. From the human standpoint, it was natural for Jesus to shrink from death and pray that death's cup might escape his lips. "With loud cries and tears," he agonized about his death. To say that he was praying for his resurrection is to miss the whole point of his agony.

We may need to revise much of our thinking about prayer. Is it not radically different from a convenient fire escape, or from a coin-operated machine that automatically drops the goods down when a coin is inserted? Someone says: "I prayed and prayed and God didn't hear me. Nothing. Silence. It was as though he was not there!" Yes, but what did you pray for? Only eradication of that dreaded disease? Did you pray also for comfort and stamina and faith—faith in the midst of shadows, faith enough to see it through, faith in God as a good Father who, seeing all things from beginning to end, knows what is best for his children? Humbly, we must pray the prayer that Jesus prayed, "Not my will, but thy will be done."

3. What does this passage teach us about the love of God? Who believes that God sent Jesus to the cross because

he did not love him? The truth is that God's love is not human love, and that the love of God reacts sometimes in a way that we do not expect. God loves us unconditionally. But because he is God, his love includes his divine wisdom. Jesus, though Son, had to pass through suffering. We, too, and our loved ones, will confront death. (We surely will, unless Christ comes before then.) But God is there, and he loves us. And Christ has experienced it all.

> Thou art of this world, Christ. Thou know'st it all;
> Thou know'st our evens, our morns, our red and gray;
> How moons, and hearts, and seasons rise and fall;
> How we grow weary plodding on the way.*

Knowing that he was flesh, knowing that he knows, let us be grateful for the merciful high priest, our Beautiful Savior.

---

*George MacDonald, *Diary of an Old Soul: 366 Writings for Devotional Reflection,* devotional for November 1 (Minneapolis: Augsburg, 1975), 112.

QUESTIONS

1. State and give the meaning of the four "let-us-es" in chapter 4.
2. In 4:14–16, explain the following: "passed through the heavens," "confidence," "draw near," and "throne of grace."
3. What does it mean to *you* that Christ has been tempted in every respect, just as human beings are tempted (4:15)? Why does the author of Hebrews bring this out?
4. List and discuss the qualifications of the Jewish high priest (5:1–4) and how perfectly Christ meets these qualifications.
5. What do Christ's "loud cries and tears" (5:7) point back to? What does this imply about Christ and his priesthood?
6. Summarizing 5:1–10, what great truths are taught here?

6

Exhortation: On to Mature Teaching

Hebrews 5:11—6:20

Let us . . . go on to maturity.
HEBREWS 6:1

We come to the grand middle chapters of Hebrews (5:11–10:39). The subject is the high priesthood of Christ, as shown by the author's announcement of his next theme: Christ "being designated by God a high priest after the order of Melchizedek" (5:10). This is the theme the author places before his readers in the central section of his letter. The importance of this theme is expressed by the centrality of its location and by its length, which comprises about two-fifths of the work.

By now it should be clear that Hebrews is very logically arranged and well organized. In 5:10 the author of Hebrews states his third major theme: CHRIST, A PRIEST

LIKE MELCHIZEDEK. Altogether, including those that lie ahead, we find five announcement themes:

1. CHRIST, SUPERIOR TO THE ANGELS (1:4)
2. CHRIST, A MERCIFUL AND FAITHFUL HIGH PRIEST (2:17)
3. CHRIST, A PRIEST LIKE MELCHIZEDEK (5:10)
4. PEOPLE OF FAITH (10:39)
5. PEACEFUL FRUIT OF RIGHTEOUSNESS (12:11)

There are a number of wonderful verses in Hebrews. If as you study you try to remember (memorize?) these key verses, you will always have in mind the leading thoughts and basic outline of the letter.

The first priority in understanding Scripture is that it be read by paragraphs and chapters, not one verse at a time. This entire midsection of Hebrews should be read and reread with a view to the message overall. If we read over it several times, perhaps we can begin to see the distinctive features of this section. They may be outlined as follows:

a. Exhortation: on to mature teaching (5:11–6:20)
b. Christ, like Melchizedek (7:1–28)
c. Christ, the source of eternal salvation (8:1–10:18; cf. 5:9)
d. Exhortation: a call to draw near (10:19–39)

Notice the symmetry and fine balance evident in the section, and notice also how this central section focuses on Christ as priest and his redemptive sacrifice.

"Stereo" Food (5:11–14)

Before exploring further the subject of Christ as high priest, the author speaks again to his readers and admonishes them. This is now his third pause for exhortation. The three exhortation passages thus far may be summarized as follows:

1. Exhortation against **d**rifting from God's word (2:1–4).
2. Exhortation against **d**isbelieving God's word (3:7–4:16).
3. Exhortation against **d**ullness toward God's word (5:11–6:20).

As throughout, the danger is of making light of the ever-to-be-revered divine message.

The author knows his readers well and knows their perilous condition. Earlier (3:12), he has spoken of this condition as that which might lead them to "apostasy," a total and final falling away from Christ. In the next section, he will describe this apostasy again with its irreversible consequences (6:4–8). What he fears is not so much a sudden departure from faith but rather that his readers might slip bit by bit into a state of spiritual unconcern and then give up Christ altogether.

About the Melchizedek-Christ type of priesthood, the author says, he "has much to say," although it is a subject that is "hard to explain." We today are ready to agree that "Melchizedek" is a difficult topic, since often we even have trouble with his name. (From now on let's shorten it and simply call him "Mel.") But the author is thinking not about Mel alone, but how Christ is a high priest like Mel. He wants to lead his readers to the higher ground of the priesthood of Christ, not a deep subject in itself, but one made difficult because they had become "dull of hearing." Their problem was not that they were "slow learners" (contrary to the NIV), but that over the years they had slipped into a lukewarm attitude toward hearing God's word.

The first readers of this letter had been Christians for a considerable period of time, long enough for them to be able to receive "advanced" instruction. This is what the author refers to when he says that by now, "you ought to be teachers." He is not saying that each and every one of them was expected to be a teacher. Instead, he is using "teachers" to stand for those who think and act maturely. In other words, he says that they are acting not as adults but as infants. They need to be taught all over again "the elementary truths of God's word." They need a diet of milk.

On the other hand, "solid food" is for grownups. We are familiar with the word for "solid." It is the Greek word *stereos*, the word we use for "stereophonic" sound. A "stereo" produces three-dimensional, solid sound. And "stereo" food is the very thing they should have.

While an infant is "unskilled" or "inexperienced" in the "word of righteousness" (God's word which leads to right conduct), "solid food is for the mature" (v. 14). Who are the mature? "Those who have their faculties trained by practice to distinguish good from evil." The "faculties" ordinarily refer to the five physical senses, but here stand for the ability to perceive spiritually. One develops the spiritual senses by practice *(gegymnasmena),* as an athlete does in a gymnasium. Such repetitive practice for the Christian enables him/her to distinguish what is spiritually good and what is spiritually bad (in context, especially, good from bad teachings).

What is the author saying? That we must not be milk Christians? Not exactly. A diet of milk, the ABCs of the gospel, is indispensable for the newborn. Yet it is worth pondering how many Christians today are satisfied to remain ever as they began, content with nothing more than introductory truths. For them, and for the original readers, the author offers "stereo" food—a fuller, deeper, maturing vision of Christ and of him as our heavenly high priest.

Pressing on to Maturity (6:1—3)

The next few verses, indeed down through 6:8, con-
nect directly with the foregoing. Verse 1 involves a twofold
exhortation: "Let us leave . . . and go on." That is, let us
leave behind the elementary teachings pertaining to
Christ, and let us go on to more advanced teaching concerning his priesthood. If the readers will truly understand the meaning of Christ's priesthood and his atoning
sacrifice, this will be enough to keep them from apostasy.
Once and for all, they must decide. Is Aaron (and his
descendants) high priest or is Christ? And who offers the
real sacrifice for sins?

A foundation already laid does not need to be laid again
and again. The author lists six items as examples of basics
that need no further emphasis.

1. Repentance from "dead works." Repentance is much
more than sorrow for sin. It is a turning from the "dead
works" of sin (cf. 9:14), a renunciation of the former life
that leads to death (cf. Rom. 6:23).

2. Faith in God. In Hebrews, faith is always active, as
demonstrated in chapter 11. It is not enough to leave the
dead works of sin, but there must be the positive turning
to God in faith.

3. Baptisms. The term is plural and is the general word
for "washings" (cf. 9:10; Mark 7:4). Jewish and pagan
washings would need to be distinguished from Christian
baptism, and so the author uses the general instead of the
specific term for baptism.

4. Laying on of hands. This was essentially a Jewish
custom, generally either to appoint someone to a task
(Acts 6:6; 13:3), or to confer a blessing (Matt. 19:15),
including that of healing (Mark 5:23) or of the Holy Spirit
(Acts 8:17; 19:6).

5. Resurrection of the dead. Jesus and the apostles
taught the resurrection of all the dead (John 5:28–29;

Acts 4:2), a basic truth that the author's readers readily acknowledged.

6. Eternal judgment. The preaching of the resurrection also involved the preaching of impending judgment (Acts 17:31) with its lasting consequences.

This list of elementary truths is not a complete list, but the author is anxious to move his readers on to more mature teaching "if God permits."

A Warning against Apostasy (6:4—8)

This is by no means the first warning in Hebrews, but it is (together with 10:26–31) the most startling and severe. The warning is stated in a long, impressive sentence beginning with the words, "For it is impossible . . ." "For" connects with that which precedes: if the readers do not go forward in their understanding of Christ, the alternative is to fall back, presumably to their prior Judaism, and commit apostasy.

"Impossible" (see 6:18; 10:4; 11:6) stresses that for some there can be no bringing back to repentance. Who cannot be renewed? Clause by clause, the author describes them. They have been "once enlightened," a reference to their conversion (cf. 10:32) when they came to a "knowledge of the truth" (10:26). They have "tasted the heavenly gift" and have "shared in the Holy Spirit" (NIV). "Taste" denotes a full experience (cf. 2:9), not just to taste with the lips. They had personally experienced salvation and had received the Spirit. Also, they had "tasted" the good word of God and "the powers of the age to come." "Age to come" is an expression from an Old Testament point of view, referring to the coming days of the Messiah.

With such vivid descriptions of the conversion experience, it is well to ask what the author intends in these verses. Is he speaking hypothetically or factually? The Revised Standard Version and New International Version render the next clause conditionally, "if they then commit apostasy" or "if they then fall away." On the other hand, the New Revised Standard Version states the case as a fact and reads simply, "and then have fallen away," which is similar to how the American Standard Version and New English Bible put it. Although it is possible to translate the clause as a condition, it is better to recognize here a series of descriptive clauses and render them all in the past. In other words, the author seems to be recounting what has happened to others and warning his readers that the same thing can happen to them. Clearly, there would be no need for alarm if falling away were not possible.

The author goes on to set forth the hardened condition of apostates: they "crucify the Son of God all over again" (NIV) and "hold him up to contempt." This is why it is impossible to restore them. They abuse him who is "the Son of God." They nail him to the cross again and publicly shame him. They do not simply disbelieve him, but they denounce and disgrace him before the world.

The danger of apostasy is illustrated by two kinds of soil, with widely different results. On one hand is land, well watered and cultivated, which "receives a blessing from God." On the other is worthless land of "thorns and thistles." It is "near to being cursed" and is "to be burned." That is, God's judgment on it is only a matter of time. As a farmer burns off his unproductive field, so the end of the apostate is certain destruction.

The whole passage presents a somber picture. It needs to be emphasized that the subject of the passage is *apostasy*. The author is not speaking of sins of temptation or of human weakness. Peter denied Christ, yet he repented of his sin. He fell short, but he did not fall away. It is one thing to commit separate acts of sin and seek forgiveness. It is an entirely different thing to "deliberately keep on sinning" (10:26 NIV), and go so far that one cannot return to God. Such a person *cannot* be saved because he is no longer able to repent.

We should also emphasize the meaning of this passage for its original readers. If they are wobbling between things Jewish and Christian, they must face the peril of their situation. So the author brings them to the edge of the cliff in order that they might look below and see the dismal end of apostates.

A Word of Encouragement (6:9—12)

Later, the author will return to the subject of apostasy, especially in 10:26–31 and in 12:12–29. That he has dealt with the topic previously and will do so again clearly shows apostasy to be possible for his readers. Nevertheless, he hastens to add here that in their case he is quite confident of "better things . . . that accompany salvation" (NIV). Remember he knows them well. He wants to encourage them. With a special touch, for the first and only time, he calls them "beloved." He assures them God will not "overlook" their work and love shown in the past (cf. 10:32–34). Notice that "love" and "work" go together. To love is to do. They had served "the saints," God's people; and they were still serving them. "Serve" (Greek, *diakoneo*) is a technical term for the beautiful, "loving service" enjoined on all Christians (see Matt. 25:31–40). The author is convinced that anyone who demonstrates such love to others must also have a measure of active faith, the very opposite of the apostate whose field yields only thorns and thistles.

But the exhortation is that the readers may press on. "We desire each one of you to show the same earnestness in realizing the full assurance of hope until the end." The word "desire" expresses an intense longing. He so much wants them to have "the full assurance" (cf. 10:22) of hope. They have love. They have faith to some extent. They lack assurance and hope. Had their attraction to Judaism robbed them of their assurance? And what about us? Are we so carried away with the world that we no longer have that "blessed assurance"?

Hebrews 6:13 ends the section begun in 5:11. As the author earlier had described his readers as "dull" (*nothroi,* 5:11), so now he urges them that they not be "sluggish" (*nothroi*). To the contrary, they are to be "imitators of those who through faith and patience inherit the promises." The thought of imitation occurs again in 13:7, and again in connection with faith. Through faith that perseveres they, like their illustrious forefathers (cf. Heb. 11), should lay claim to what is promised. The mention of "promises" leads the way to the next paragraph.

Standing on God's Promises (6:13—20)

We have read and pondered the great passage on God's rest in 4:1–13. His rest is still open, for "the promise" of entering it still remains (4:1). The word "promise" (noun and verb) occurs eighteen times in Hebrews, more than in any other New Testament book. As we go through Hebrews, we should take note of these important passages. In the paragraph before us, the author establishes the certainty of these promises and their self-evident basis for hope. Truly, the Christian stands on the promises of God. "He who promised is faithful" (10:23).

Of all those who "inherit the promises," the name of Abraham is distinctive. "When God made a promise to

Abraham, . . . he swore by himself, saying, 'Surely I will bless you and multiply you.'" To swear by God is the strongest oath possible, and so God swore by himself. The occasion referred to is that of the offering of Isaac, when God promised that Abraham's offspring would be as numberless as "the stars of heaven and as the sand which is on the seashore" (Gen. 22:17).

Earlier, much earlier, God had promised Abraham that he would make of him a great nation (Gen. 12:2). How could this be? He had no son or daughter. But he believed God and patiently waited on his promise. Twenty-five years later Isaac was born (Gen. 21:1–7), and years later he received him back from death. Through all of this, especially at the time when he was ready to sacrifice Isaac, Abraham "patiently endured" and so "obtained the promise." In Isaac he could begin to see the working out of God's promise that, in a deeper sense, would not be fulfilled until Christ came (11:13; 11:39–40).

Man (mankind) might often break his word, and so humans have to confirm their words with oaths. But God's promises depend not on us but on his faithfulness. When God spoke to Abraham, he had in view not just Abraham but particularly "the heirs of the promise." Here "the heirs" include all people of faith, whom the author will illustrate further in chapter 11.

God's mere word is enough; but to give assurance down through the centuries, he "guaranteed it by an oath" (NRSV). God's dependable word and his irrevocable oath— these are the two unchangeable things in which "it is impossible for God to lie" (v. 18 NIV). So to speak, God is doubly bound to keep his promise.

Such gracious assurance, the author says, has a grand design: that "we who have fled for refuge" might "have strong encouragement." (Remember, Hebrews is a "message of encouragement," 13:22). Christians are the very ones who have fled for "refuge," a term used figuratively for their escape to Christ from the dangers of the world.

The idea is that we have fled to Christ, our Eternal Refuge. We are to reach out toward him; we are to "seize," take hold of, grasp firmly "the hope set before us." "Hope" here, as always in Hebrews, does not refer to "our hoping," but clearly to the object of hope. It denotes what we hope for, the goal of all our anticipations and desires. "Here we have no lasting city, but we seek the city which is to come" (13:14).

We have seen that the language of Hebrews is very rhetorical. Now, in a splendidly glorious way, the author goes on to portray the nature of Christian hope. "We have this," he says, "as a sure and steadfast anchor of the soul." What an inspiring affirmation! How compelling for persecuted Christians in the first century and for every Christian today! Hope is an anchor for our lives. And it is strong and secure. Why? Because it "enters into the inner shrine behind the curtain, where Jesus has gone." Our anchor is cast *upward* where Christ is!

Although the anchor image occurs only here in the entire Bible, it was especially meaningful to early Christians. It was frequently combined with the fish symbol, and it is found numerous times in the Roman catacombs and on Christian tombs. But the anchor symbolism here is not fully worked out. Whether it is the anchor or hope itself that connects within the curtain, the general sense is the same.

Reference to "the curtain" and the "inner shrine" (literally, "the inner") points forward to chapter 9, and to the "entering" of Jesus depicted in the focal verses of the chapter (9:11–14). On the Day of Atonement the Jewish high priest passed through the "curtain" or "veil," which separated the Holy Place from the Most Holy Place. When the author speaks of Jesus as entering behind the curtain, he is not only using tabernacle imagery but he is thinking once again of Jesus as our high priest. He "has passed through the heavens" (4:14). This is high priestly language. He has entered "behind the curtain." Again, this is high priestly language. So the author means that Jesus, on going behind the curtain, has entered into the real Holy of Holies, where God is, into heaven itself (cf. 9:12, 24).

Too, Jesus has gone into heaven "as a forerunner on our behalf." The term "forerunner" was often used of a military "scout" who preceded the main army. So Jesus is our scout who has gone ahead of us in order that we may follow. Notice that the author does not say "our forerunner" but "forerunner for us." The latter expression is an allusion to his marvelous, one-time-sacrificial death as our high priest (see chapters 9–10). With this the author picks up again his main theme announced in 5:10, Christ, "a high priest after the order of Melchizedek."

With remarkable skill the author brings the readers' minds back to his subject. Having pressed them for further spiritual progress and having set before them the fatal consequences if they do not progress, he encourages them to keep on in the path of salvation. God indeed has promised, made doubly sure with his oath; and they, in a fuller sense than Abraham, are heirs of that promise. But the realization of the promise for them was still in the future. Of all things, they needed to hold on unswervingly to their hope. Hope, anchored in the eternal Christ, would enable them to ride the waves safely in the fury of the storm. But the author wants to underscore that they would have no hope at all if it were not for the priestly work of Christ in the heavenly Holy of Holies. This subject, Christ's priesthood like that of Melchizedek, which they had scorned, was the very subject they needed to hear.

QUESTIONS

1. Review and keep in mind the five "announcement themes" in Hebrews. How does the middle section of the letter relate to these themes?
2. Hebrews 5:11–6:20 is an exhortation against dullness toward God's word. How did the readers' condition give rise to the exhortation? What subject did the author want to pursue?
3. What is the meaning of "by this time you ought to be teachers" (5:12)? What is "stereo" food?
4. What occasioned the author's discussion of apostasy? How would attention to more mature teaching about Christ's priesthood keep the readers from falling away?
5. What hopeful signs does the author of Hebrews see concerning his readers (6:9–12)? How will they be able to "inherit the promises"?
6. What are the two unchangeable things in which "it is impossible for God to lie" (6:18)? How are they related to God's promises?
7. Explain how hope is an "anchor of the soul" (6:19). How does it enter "behind the curtain"?

7

Jesus, like Melchizedek

Hebrews 7:1—28

You are a priest forever, in the order of Melchizedek.

HEBREWS 7:17 NIV

So far we have seen that Jesus is a true high priest, one who has proved himself faithful to God and merciful to humankind (2:17). We have seen also that Christ meets the requirements set down for the Old Testament high priest (5:1–10), just as Aaron did. But could there be *two* high priests or *two* orders of priesthood? No! According to Moses' law, Israel could never have two spiritual heads at the same time.

The original readers, of course, knew this. But there was something that they did not know, that Scripture (Ps. 110:4) speaks of another order of priesthood, that of Melchizedek. (Remember, we're calling him

"Mel.") They must understand unequivocally that the priesthood of the sort of Mel excels in all aspects the kind of priesthood represented by Aaron. Chapters 7, 8, 9, and 10 demonstrate that what Christ offers as high priest far surpasses the best of all that Judaism could offer. The author develops his points in terms of (1) covenant, (2) sanctuary, and (3) sacrifice.

It is precisely here—and we might as well admit it— where Hebrews becomes pedantic and tedious for us. Sacrifice, sanctuary, covenant, and of all things, Mel! Certainly, we do not know much about Mel. And even if somehow Mel is connected with Christ, what does this have to do with us? Yet there are several things that we should keep in mind: (1) Priestly service and holy places were well known in the ancient world, and even Mel was a familiar figure to people of Jewish background. (2) Symbols and types are not just for the ancient mind. Types, and what they correspond with, called "antitypes," provide important links between Old and New Testaments and reflect divine anticipations of things fulfilled in Christ. (3) The subject matter in chapters 7–10 focuses our minds on Christ and what he has done for us. Once we read and grasp the meaning of these chapters, we will never be the same. Christ as high priest offered himself— the one, great, final offering for all our sins.

The concluding statement in 6:20 restates the author's announcement theme in 5:10, except for one difference: Christ has become a priest *forever*. Notice the addition of the word "forever," which also happens to be the very last word (in the Greek text) in chapter 6. Is this a gentle hint for what follows?

Suppose we read chapter 7 straight through. We will find Mel's name five times, but this is not the important thing. The emphasis is not on Mel but Christ. On the other hand, we will find one main idea that runs all through the chapter: the *foreverness* of Christ's priesthood. Look at the many ways the author brings this out, as he speaks of Christ. "He continues a priest for ever" (v. 3). "[He] has become a priest . . . by the power of an indestructible life" (v. 16). "You are a priest for ever" (v. 17; v. 21; cf. v. 8). "He holds his priesthood permanently" (v. 24). "He continues for ever" (v. 24). "He is able for all time to save" (v. 25). "He always lives to make intercession" (v. 25). "The word of the oath . . . appoints a Son who has been made perfect for ever" (v. 28).

So the main lines of chapter 7 are very clear. Now let us see how the author builds up his thoughts and lays stress on the unique and eternal nature of Christ's priesthood.

Melchizedek and Abraham (7:1—10)

Verses 1–10 form the first major division of chapter 7, shown by the repetition of key words:

Melchizedek . . . met Abraham. (v. 1)
Melchizedek met him [Abraham]. (v. 10)

These key words separate the passage off as a distinct unit and call attention to the significant meeting of Abraham and Mel.

There are only two passages in the Old Testament that mention Mel. One of these is the brief royal psalm, Psalm 110, alluded to and quoted several times already, and is yet to be expounded in the last half of this chapter. The other passage is Genesis 14:18–20, which the author now reviews and comments on.

"For this Melchizedek, king of Salem and priest of the Most High God, met Abraham returning from the slaughter of the kings and blessed him, and to him apportioned a tenth part of everything" (vv. 1–2). This is only the beginning of the long sentence which, as originally written, goes down through verse 3. Read altogether, the main thought of the sentence is "Melchizedek . . . continues a priest forever." Notice the parallel with the concluding idea of chapter 6.

> Mel is a priest who continues forever. (7:1–3)
> Christ is a priest forever. (6:20)

Going back to the end of chapter 6, the grand thought is that Christ has entered heaven and remains there as our high priest. Mel is the ideal illustration of this.

We should take time to read Genesis 14, which narrates Abraham's rout of four kings in battle. Afterward, Mel greeted and blessed Abraham. Abraham, laden with the spoils of victory, allotted Mel a tenth of them.

But who was Mel? He was "king of Salem," and his name means "king of righteousness." Further, Mel was "without father or mother or genealogy," having "neither beginning of days nor end of life." Above all, Mel is like "the Son of God" and "remains a priest for ever."

All of this is seen by the author as typical, both in what is explicitly said and what is implied.

1. Mel was a priest and so is Christ. Genesis describes Mel in exalted terms, "priest of God Most High." Mel as priest blessed Abraham. Abraham, in turn, acknowledged Mel as priest and gave him a tenth of everything.

2. Mel was a king and so is Christ. Mel as priest-king prefigured Christ as king and priest. This, as the author has shown, is the very substance of Psalm 110. Messiah is to "sit" at God's hand (Ps. 110:10—this is kingly language. Messiah is addressed as a "priest forever"—this is priestly language.

3. Mel is righteousness and peace and so is Christ. "Melchizedek" in Hebrew means "king of righteousness." Also, Mel was king of "Salem" (probably Jerusalem), which means that he was "king of peace." We are not to

think that these names are just wordplays. Names to Jewish readers were significant. They stood for the essential nature of that to which they belonged. The inference is that Mel as priest-king points to the Messiah who truly is the King of Righteousness and the Prince of Peace (cf. Ps. 72:7; Isa. 9:6–7; Rom. 5:1).

4. Mel is priest without genealogy and so is Christ. Mel is described by three thought-provoking words—"fatherless," "motherless," and "genealogyless." What does this mean? Certainly it does not mean that Mel literally had no father or mother. Mel was a real person, a real priest, a real king of a real city. Suppose we translate the terms slightly different—"father unknown," "mother unknown," and "genealogy unknown." Although Genesis is filled with genealogies, Mel seems to appear suddenly on the scene "without father or mother." He was a priest but not on the basis of his family history. Notice how this fits the context. Just a few verses later, Mel is contrasted with the Levitical priests with respect to *genealogy*. "This man," referring to Mel, who "has not their genealogy" (v. 6). Mel's priesthood rested on who he was, not on who his parents were. In this respect, again, he illustrates Christ as priest.

5. Mel's priesthood is timeless and so is Christ's. Genesis relates neither when Mel began his priesthood nor when he ended it. It does not tell about his birth or death. In this sense, then, according to the author, Mel "has neither beginning of days nor end of life." And because Christ has been from all eternity and Mel has not, Mel in reality "resembles the Son of God."

It should be emphasized that these verses, when properly understood, do not make Mel a shadowy, mysterious figure. It is true that in centuries past he has been the subject of much speculation. One of the documents of the Dead Sea Scrolls, for example, pictures him as a kind of heavenly being who executes judgment on God's enemies. Undoubtedly, both author and readers were acquainted with such views. So the author seems to be saying something like this: "We know there's a great deal of study going on concerning Mel. But if you look carefully in your Bible, you'll see that Mel points you to Christ our high priest."

The author moves on in the next verses (4–10) to demonstrate how Mel is superior to Abraham. Why do this? Because if Mel has a higher status than Abraham, by implication his priesthood must rise above any order of priests tied to Abraham. The argument can be summarized in four points.

1. Mel is superior because Abraham tithed him. "See how great he is!" Such heightened language concerning Mel suggests a lesson to be learned. Even "Abraham the patriarch" gave Mel a tenth of the booty.

Reference is now made to the Levites, because the author's ultimate concern is to contrast Mel's priesthood with that of Levi. The Levitical priests, who are descended from Abraham, "have a commandment in the law to take tithes . . . from their brethren." In other words, tithing was practiced because it was in the law (Num. 18:21–24); and tithes were received by the Levites from their equals. But in Mel's case, he was tithed not by an equal but by the great Abraham. Besides, Abraham tithed Mel not because he had to but because he wanted to. Thus Abraham's action put Mel's priesthood in a different category altogether.

2. Mel is superior because Mel "blessed him who had the promises." Notice the implied contrast between Abraham who had the promises and the Levites who had the law. It is axiomatic, "beyond all dispute," that the superior blesses the inferior. ("Bless the Lord" is not an exception, for in such expressions "bless" means "give thanks to" or "praise.")

3. Mel is superior because he is immortal. The Levitical priests collect the tithe as dying men, but Mel has an immortal life. Since Genesis says nothing about his death, in this sense "it is testified" in Scripture that "he lives."

4. Mel is superior because even Levi paid tithes to him. This point is made figuratively. Levi was a great-grandson of Abraham. He was in the body (literally "in the loins") of his ancestor when Mel met him. Levi, then, gave a tithe to Mel and thus confessed the inferiority of his priesthood to that of Mel.

The Inadequacy of the Old Priesthood (7:11—19)

The words "perfect" and "perfection" supply the key to this section: "If perfection could be attained through the Levitical priesthood . . ." (v. 11 NIV). "For the law made nothing perfect" (v. 19). The leading thought is clear, stated at the opening of this section and at the close, that the law could not bring perfection. We have previously discussed the word "perfect" in 2:10 and 5:9. As we have seen, we cannot possibly understand the term in Hebrews unless we recognize its "priestly" sense. Earlier it is used of Christ, here with reference to his people. As a priest had to be "perfected" in order to approach God, so there had to be something to "perfect" God's people and make possible a right relationship with him. The law could never do this. It was woefully insufficient because it had no real sacrifice for sin (9:9; 10:4).

While we may think of the Mosaic law as also including the priesthood, the author's thought is exactly the opposite. For him the priesthood was the foundation of everything. The law could not function without it. So if "a change in the priesthood" has occurred, there must be also "a change in the law" (v. 12). What law? Specifically, in context, the law concerning priesthood. Read the next verse. "For the one of whom these things are spoken"— Jesus in Psalm 110—"belonged to another tribe."

It was a matter of public record, reflected in the genealogies of Matthew and Luke, that "our Lord was descended from Judah" (v. 14). It was equally well known that Moses allotted no priestly service to that tribe. This means that Jesus could never be an earthly high priest. If he is to be a priest at all, his priesthood must be of a different order. Indeed, this is the very message of Psalm 110, which promises in the likeness of Mel a priest "for ever." This cannot apply to any of the Levitical priests. They were all mortal. Even Mel was not literally a priest forever, for as a human being, he, too, died. One and one only "has become" (and remains) a priest "by the power of an indestructible life" (v. 16). Death had no hold on him (cf. Acts 2:24). Risen to heaven at God's right hand, his heavenly life and heavenly priesthood are indestructible.

The section on the inadequacy of the Levitical priesthood is now brought to a conclusion, with a statement of both negative and positive results. "On the one hand, a former commandment is set aside because of its weakness and uselessness" (v. 18). The "former commandment," in context, is the requirement that based priesthood on ancestry (v. 16).

Three things in particular are said about this former commandment.

1. It was weak. The whole Levitical arrangement was very limited in what it could achieve. Contrast its "weakness" with the "power" of Christ's "indestructible life" (v. 16).

2. It was useless. What a strong word! Immediately we ask why God would set up something that was "useless." Again, we have to see the meaning in context. The Levitical order never accomplished what we expect priests to be able to do. On the Day of Atonement, when the high priest entered before God, the people had to stand outside. That was always the case in the Levitical ceremony. Always the people had to stand back. The truth is that the Levitical law, with all its pomp and circumstance, "made

nothing [or no one] perfect" (v. 19). It never brought anyone close to God for worship.

3. It was set aside. Because it was weak and useless to
effect its purpose, the priestly arrangement had to be "set
aside." The term here is a legal term, appropriate for the
priestly law being discussed. It means to "cancel" or "dis-
annul," just as a decree is annulled or a debt is wiped out.
The author does not hesitate to say that the Levitical law
has been canceled. It is out-of-date, over, finished! It has
been wiped away!

The eternal priesthood of Christ, like that of Mel,
means, on one hand and stated negatively, the annulment
of the old. "On the other hand," stated positively, it means
"a better hope is introduced, through which we draw near
to God" (v. 19). The "former commandment" and the "better hope" are poles apart. Christ is the one who brings not
a better law or better commandment but a better *hope.*
Hope shines brightly all through Hebrews (3:6; 6:11, 18;
cf. 10:23; 11:1). Jesus Christ has bestowed on us what the
priestly law could not do. No longer do we have to stand
at a distance, but through him we can "draw near to God."

The Supremacy of the New Priesthood (7:20—28)

Verses 20–28 make up the final section in this chapter. Let us see if we can discover what the main thought
here is. Notice the word "oath" is stated in verse 21 and
is restated in verse 28. That is the key word that gives us
the key idea in these verses. Christ has become our high
priest *with an oath.*

All along the author has been quoting from Psalm 110.
In the strictest sense this psalm is an "oracle," a direct
message from God. It opens with the very significant
words, "The Lord says." The word for "says" is unusual
and denotes an "inspired utterance." So this psalm, which

in a unique way claims to be from God, is the very psalm used by the author to prove Christ as king and priest.

Earlier, as we have seen, God affirmed his covenant with Abraham by an oath (6:13–17). Now, in the words of Psalm 110, he addresses the Son: "The Lord has sworn and will not change his mind, 'You are a priest forever'" (v. 21 NRSV). God never swore this concerning the Levites. They were priests without an oath. But God made a solemn oath to Christ. This makes his priesthood superior and confirms that it will last forever.

God's oath also makes Jesus "the guarantee of a better covenant" (NRSV). Here for the first time we read the word "covenant," and in the next few chapters we will see how much "better" it is. It is enough now to say that the better covenant especially deals with sin. God says that he will remember our sins no more. How marvelous! Yet how can we be sure? Christ himself is the "surety" or "guarantee" of the better covenant. He is the one who personally guarantees that the terms of the covenant will be fully met.

And there is more. "The former priests were many in number . . . but [Christ] holds his priesthood permanently" (vv. 23–24). "Many" suggests ongoing ineffectiveness. The Old Testament priests died, one after another. According to the Jewish historian Josephus, there were eighty-three high priests from the time of Aaron to the destruction of the temple in A.D. 70.

By contrast, Christ lives forever. He will never need to pass on his priesthood to someone else. This means "he is able for all time to save those who draw near to God through him" (v. 25). Christ saves "for all time," or "to the uttermost" (KJV). Saves whom? Those who "draw near" to God. He is able to save, if we are willing. Save how? In the sense that he "always lives to make intercession" for us. He pleads our case "at God's right hand" (Rom. 8:34; cf. 1 John 2:1). Even in heaven he lives for us.

The remaining verses summarize and point forward and, at the same time, wonderfully praise the majestic Christ. "It was fitting [the same word as in 2:10] that we should have such a high priest" (v. 26). That is, Christ perfectly fits our needs. He lived a sinless life—"holy, blameless, unstained." He now lives a glorious life—"separated from sinners, exalted above the heavens." The latter expression is but another way of saying that Christ is in the presence of God (cf. 4:14). There—in locale, not in his disposition—he is set apart from sinners.

Christ is not only the perfect priest, but he is the perfect sacrifice. All the previous high priests had "to offer sacrifices daily" (v. 27). On the Day of Atonement the Jewish high priest had to offer sacrifice first for himself and for his family, and then for all the people (cf. 9:6–7; Lev. 16:6–34). There were also daily sacrifices offered by the priests. It is possible here, however, that "day after day" (NRSV) refers to every day when the high priest officiated, that is, Atonement Day. But how different Christ is. He offered the one perfect offering—"once for all . . . he offered up himself."

Verse 28 concludes by restating some of the main points in verses 11–27. Again, notice the marked contrasts between: (1) "the law" and "the word of the oath"; (2) "men" and "a Son"; and (3) the Levitical high priests "in their weakness" and the Son as high priest "who has been made perfect forever." The term that so aptly describes the whole Levitical arrangement is "weakness" (v. 19; cf. 5:2). But the Son, who never knew the weakness of sin, went to the cross and so has been fully equipped as high priest for us—"made perfect forever."

Let us look back over this rather intricate chapter. Three persons or groups stand out.

1. Melchizedek. Melchizedek (Mel), whose priesthood is the oldest known in the Biblical record (Gen. 14), is

the ideal for all priests. Suited for kings, not based on flesh and blood, his priesthood is like that of the Son of God. And if the original readers have any question about whose priesthood is superior, that of Aaron or of Mel, Scripture itself supplies the answer. The historical narrative clearly demonstrates the superiority of Mel over Abraham and also over his great-grandson Levi.

2. The Levitical priests. Oh, if their many sacrifices could have achieved their purpose! Whatever the priestly law was designed to do, it had ultimately failed. An old car might get you around the block, but not carry you around the world. Something else, some other kind of vehicle, is absolutely necessary. In the case of priesthood, only one succeeds and gets us all the way into the presence of God.

3. Jesus. Remember, the subject of chapter 7 is not Mel but Christ. Mel serves as an illustration of Christ and then fades from view. Verses 20–28 form the climactic section, and here the name "Jesus" appears for the first time in the chapter. "Jesus has become the guarantee of a better covenant" (7:22 NRSV).

Jesus is supremely able to guarantee this covenant because of his "indestructible life" (v. 16). He always lives (v. 25). The new covenant, which especially offers forgiveness of sins, will last as long as he will last. There is more. Because he never dies, because he never has a priest to succeed him, he will always be there, in heaven, for each of us.

And Jesus is not weak like others. If you go to some earthly priest, he might first have to put himself right with God before he can see you. Not so with the One who is "holy, blameless, unstained" (v. 26). In character, he stands apart from us. As a sacrifice, he died for us "once for all" (v. 27). "He offered himself," "He offered himself," "He offered himself"—it is an ascending refrain in the chapters that follow. "Beautiful Savior!"

QUESTIONS

1. Why is Christ a priest like Melchizedek an important subject for *us*?
2. What is the leading idea of chapter 7? Trace this
   idea through the chapter and list the verses that
   express it.
3. List the similarities between Christ's priesthood and
   that of Melchizedek. In what sense is Melchizedek
   a priest "without father or mother" (7:3)?
4. What tribe was Christ from? What does this imply
   about his priesthood (cf. 8:4)? How are verses 11–14
   of chapter 7 tied to one another?
5. What is the "former commandment" that has been
   canceled (7:18)? What is it contrasted with?
6. In what sense does Christ guarantee the "better
   covenant" (7:22)?

8

Jesus: Better Ministry, Better Promises

Hebrews 8:1—13

The ministry Jesus has received is as superior . . . as the covenant . . . founded on better promises.

HEBREWS 8:6 NIV

When we come to chapter 8, the first thing we notice is that it is much shorter than chapter 7. Actually, it is the beginning of a more lengthy section that goes down to 10:18. Broadly speaking, chapters 5–7 deal with the *person* of Christ as "high priest"; chapters 8–10 focus on the *ministry* of Christ as "high priest."

But what is this ministry? How and where is it carried on? To answer these questions, we must sit quietly and allow the author to explain. No, he does much more than "explain." He pours heart and soul into his triumphant presentation of Christ's once-for-all offering of himself for sin—how the Son "has been made perfect for ever" (7:28).

The Heavenly Ministry (8:1 — 6)

This new section opens with what appears to be a summary: "Now the point in what we are saying is this." But the author only briefly mentions that "we have such a high priest," the one who is "seated at the right hand" of God's throne in heaven. Then, continuing to speak of Christ, he introduces a new theme by saying that this Christ in heaven conducts his priestly duties in heaven. That is, he is "a [priestly] minister in the sanctuary" in the real Holy of Holies erected not by mortals but by the Lord. Thus we have in 8:1–2 not just a summary, but an important advance in the author's argument. Indeed, it is his main point, which is yet to be worked out. And the point is that Christ is the real priest in the only real place where sin can be dealt with, in heaven, in the presence of God. This is only stated here in an introductory way, awaiting further development especially in two grand sections in chapter 9 (vv. 11–14, 23–28).

It is the chief function of the high priest to make offering for sin (cf. 5:1). Since Jesus is the supreme high priest, the author reasons that it is essential that he, too, "have something to offer" (v. 3). What that "something" is the author does not define now. He writes as though he wants his readers to think about it awhile, although he has already stated it (7:27) and will explain it in more detail. For the present he only wants to leave with his readers the thought that Christ had to make an offering.

Of course, that offering has in fact been made. Historically, it took place on earth—a thing of the past, finished—and so Christ took his seat in heaven. Yet spiritually speaking, in priestly symbolism and from the standpoint of eternity, though Christ died on earth, his offering was made in heaven. On earth he was not a priest. He did not belong to the correct tribe (7:13–14). Besides, on earth there were no vacancies, for Levitical priests were still offering "gifts according to the law" (v. 4).

We have seen that much of chapter 7 concerns the contrast of Christ and Levi. That contrast continues. Christ sits; the Levites stand. Christ ministers in heaven in the true tent. They serve on earth in a sanctuary that is no more than "a copy and shadow of the heavenly" one. The terms "copy" and "shadow" merge in one—a vague copy, a mere hint or suggestion of the heavenly reality. Still, everything having to do with the imperfect copy had to be made "according to the pattern" shown Moses on Mount Sinai.

We must keep in mind what the author is posing before his readers. The Jews delighted so much in their temple. To be privileged to travel to Jerusalem, to see the temple in all its splendor, with its beautiful stones, magnificent architecture, and sacred courts, for devout Jews, both in and outside of Palestine, no experience in all of life compared with this. But the author is emphatically declaring that there is something better than this. What? The session of Christ at the right hand of God in the real sanctuary! The tabernacle in the desert, and the Jerusalem temple by implication, were only vague shadows of the reality in heaven.

Therefore, there is a vast difference between the earthly and heavenly tabernacles. This prompts the author to make both a concluding statement and one that leads into his next discussion. Now "Christ has obtained a ministry which is as much more excellent than the old as the covenant he mediates is better" (v. 6). The word "ministry" is used in the same sense as "minister" in verse 2; both refer to Christ's ministry as our heavenly priest. The statement is in the "how much better" form, significant in Hebrews. Christ is "so much better" than the angels

(1:4). His covenant and his ministry are "so much better" than the old (8:6). His offered blood is "so much better" than the blood of goats and bulls (9:13–14). His blood speaks "better" than the blood of Abel (12:24).

The statement contains also a different level of comparison between Christ's better priestly ministry and his better covenant. The first inextricably involves the second, for a better ministry demands a better covenant. Indeed, the minister is the mediator. Christ is our high priestly minister and God's mediator.

Ordinarily, we think of a mediator as a go-between who stands on neutral ground and brings the contracting parties together. Certainly, Christ is our mediator. In Hebrews, however, his mediating work on our behalf is as high priest. But with reference to the (new) covenant, his function is not the same. Where the covenant is concerned, he is primarily God's representative or agent.

This is true because of the nature of the divine covenant. In the New Testament a special word is used for "covenant" *diatheke,* a term which in itself indicates that God alone lays down its conditions. Although we may make covenants or contracts as equals, this is never the case with God. In covenants with frail human beings, it is always God who stipulates and requires. God's part is to say that this is the way it is going to be. Our part, if we wish—and God never compels us against our wills—is simply to nod our heads and agree. Christ's role is to enter in and pledge that God will keep his part of the agreement. Christ guarantees the new covenant (7:22). He has made himself personally responsible for it. By his death he secures the forgiveness of sins promised in the new covenant.

Consequently, the author adds, continuing to speak of this covenant, that "it is enacted on better promises." Notice, again, the word "better." Better covenant, better promises! Previously the author has drawn attention to God's wonderful, certain promises (4:1; 6:12, 13, 15, 17;

7:6). And as we go on to read more about the new covenant, we want to look for the promises of this covenant and how the author unfolds them.

The New Covenant (8:7—13)

A better covenant with better promises implies the inadequacy of the previous covenant. "For if that first covenant had been faultless, there would have been no occasion for a second." This in a nutshell states the author's contention. The Levitical priests and sacrifices were "weak and useless" in the sense that they could not bring a person near God (7:18–19). And where in the old covenant was there a place for Christ? It was God, then, who censured the first covenant and replaced it with the second. Notice that the opening and closing statements of this section declare the temporary character of the old covenant.

The old covenant was no more than a brief setup that would have to give way to something better. This was very clear even in the time of the prophet Jeremiah. Six centuries before Christ, he saw that the nation of Judah would fall to the invading armies of Babylon. Judah had sinned; it had broken its covenant with God. It would be snuffed out, and its beautiful temple would be reduced to rubble.

But Jeremiah looked beyond all of this to the time when God would establish a new relationship with his people. "The days will come, says the Lord, when I will establish a new covenant with the house of Israel and with the house of Judah" (v. 8). The quotation, from Jeremiah 31:31–34, is the only passage in the Old Testament that specifically speaks of a "new covenant." This covenant would be radically different. It would not be like the covenant, God says, "that I made with their forefathers when I took them by the hand to lead them out of Egypt" (v. 9 NIV).

That covenant failed, first and foremost, because Israel failed. They "did not continue in my covenant, and so I paid no heed to them, says the Lord."

The author, as he continues to quote Jeremiah, describes the essential nature of the new covenant.

1. It is a covenant of assurance. "This is the covenant that I will make with the house of Israel after those days, says the Lord." The emphasis here and throughout the quotation is on what God will do. Six times God says "I will": "*I will* establish a new covenant," "This is the covenant *I will* make," "*I will* put my laws," "*I will* be their Lord," "*I will* be merciful," and "*I will* remember their sins no more." The new covenant does not primarily depend on us. We have our part in it, as we shall see. But in the final analysis, its execution rests on God and not on any one or all of us. God has promised to fulfill it. The new covenant will never be broken or displaced. This is certain and wonderfully reassuring.

2. It is a covenant of obedience. "I will put my laws into their minds, and write them on their hearts, and I will be their God, and they shall be my people" (v. 10). Set in poetic parallelism, this is beautiful covenant language. The old covenant at Sinai required obedience and offered the people a close relationship with God (Exod. 19:5–6; Lev. 26:12). Yet that covenant consisted of external commands, written on tables of stone. By contrast, the new covenant is written within, on the human heart.

But what does it really mean to have God's laws written on our hearts? In plain terms it means that *we must obey God.* In Hebrew thought, a person thinks and feels and purposes with the heart. The heart is the place of the will. If the law is written on our own hearts, we will have the will to obey it.

Several passages in the Old Testament make this abundantly clear.

For this commandment which I command you this day is not too hard for you, neither is it far off. . . . But the word is very near you; it is in your mouth and in your heart, *so that you can do it.* (Deut. 30:11–14, emphasis added)

And I will give them one heart, and put a new spirit within them; I will take the stony heart out of their flesh and give them a heart of flesh, that they may walk in my statutes and keep my ordinances *and obey them.* (Ezek. 11:19–20, emphasis added)

Burnt offering and sin offering thou has not required. Then I said, "Lo, I come . . . I delight to *do* thy will, O my God; thy law is *within my heart.*" (Ps. 40:6–8, emphasis added)

So there is a direct connection between obedience and what is in the heart. Psalm 40 is the classic passage here. Notice that this is the very passage which is quoted later and is applied to Christ's offering of himself (10:5–10). Because God's law was so deeply stamped within him, inscribed on his heart, Christ could say in the highest sense—"Lo, I have come to do thy will, O God."

The idea of a covenant of obedience continues on in the next verse: "And they shall not teach every one his fellow [literally, fellow-citizen or fellow-townsman] or every one his brother, saying, 'Know the Lord,' for all shall know me, from the least of them to the greatest" (v. 11). For those in the new covenant relationship, God writes his law on their hearts. This being so, God's covenant people do not need to be taught.

It follows that God's children do not need to go about saying to one another, "Know the Lord." Automatically, they do God's will. "Know" in the Biblical sense often means "to know and do." For example, in Hosea 4:6, God declares, "My people are destroyed for lack of knowledge." What does this mean? Verses 1–2 in the same chapter clarify: "There is no faithfulness or kindness, and no knowledge of God in the land; there is swearing, lying, killing, stealing, and committing adultery." That is, those who have no knowledge of God are those who violate God's law. If so, then the opposite is also true—to know God is to know and do his will. To put it another way, God's people have God's law within them. They know him, and they keep his law. (Cf. Jer. 5:4–5; Matt. 7:21–23; John 7:17; 8:32; 17:3.)

3. It is a covenant of grace. "For I will be merciful toward their iniquities, and I will remember their sins no more" (v. 12). Let us be sure that we not overlook the little word "for." It connects with the previous verses and shows clearly that forgiveness of sins is the basis of all the blessings in the new covenant. Indeed, this is the very heart of the new covenant, as the quotation of Jeremiah 31 later indicates (10:16–18). Forgiveness of sins did not underlie the old covenant. This, above all, as the author will show, is what the old regime could not secure (9:9; 10:11).

But written in the terms of the new covenant is God's promise of pardon. Our sins are fully forgiven and forgotten. Instead of "a reminder of sin year after year" (10:3), God remembers sin no more at all (10:17). Of course, this remarkable promise of forgiveness, this wonderful covenant of his grace, is only through Christ and his sacrifice (9:11–14, 28; 10:12–14; 13:12).

In the author's view, however, the prophecy of Jeremiah comprised something in addition. It was for him total proof that God had dated the old covenant and had made it a thing of the past. "In speaking of a new covenant he treats the first as obsolete. And what is becoming obsolete and growing old is ready to vanish away" (v. 13). Notice the word "obsolete" occurs twice. First, it refers to something that is past. This is made clear in the New International Version and in the New Revised Standard

Version which render here: "he has made the first one obsolete." God himself antiquated it. It could no longer serve his purpose.

Second, "obsolete" is used as a present participle ("becoming obsolete") and points to something that is still present. What can the author possibly mean? How can a thing be both past and present? The simple explanation is that God had already declared the first covenant as old and had canceled it. This must be the case if, on one hand, the Levitical procedure was weak and ineffective (7:19), and if, on the other hand, Christ is now installed as our high priest in heaven. Nevertheless, in point of fact, as the author was writing, the Levitical sacrifices were still being offered at the temple in Jerusalem. Yet as a vapor appears for a moment and then vanishes (James 4:14), so the author sees that the decadent system of Judaism was "ready to vanish away." Historically speaking, it did vanish as a vapor with the destruction of Jerusalem by the Romans in A.D. 70.

The new covenant perfectly fulfills the terms of an ideal covenant. God had this in mind from the time of Abraham. At Sinai he sought to establish his covenant with Israel, but Israel disdained it. They did not keep their part of the bargain. Now God has provided a new and better covenant for his people. He is theirs, and they are his. Engraved within them is the delight to do God's will. They know him and walk in his ways. And forevermore they have the forgiveness of their sins.

Christ is in heaven for them, their great high priest. He ministers in the real sanctuary above, where God is and where real forgiveness takes place.

QUESTIONS

1. How does the opening of chapter 8 provide a further step in the argument concerning Christ's priesthood?
2. What does it mean that Christ is a "minister in the sanctuary" (8:2)? What is his ministry that is "much more excellent" (8:6)?
3. Explain how Christ is the mediator of the new covenant (8:6). What is the meaning of the word "covenant"?
4. What passage in the Old Testament speaks of a "new covenant"? How is the new covenant radically different from the old one?
5. In what sense is the new covenant written on our hearts?
6. What is the wonderful promise especially offered in the new covenant?

9

Jesus, the Better Sacrifice: Part 1

Hebrews 9:1 — 28

. . . the heavenly things themselves with better sacrifices . . .

Hebrews 9:23

Several things need to be said before we go further.

1. In terms of content, all of Hebrews 9:1–10:18 belongs together.

2. Before beginning, we should take the time to read this section as a whole. We may even have to read it several times and perhaps in several different translations. Actually, this is the best approach to take whenever we come to a new section of Scripture.

3. With this study we conclude the grand middle section on Christ the high priest. Chapter 8 through 10:18 depicts the heavenly ministry of our high priest and

emphasizes more than anything else the heavenly offering of himself. Take a careful look at the key terms in this section and how they occur again and again:

Offer: (8:3, 4; 9:7, 9, 14, 25, 28; 10:1, 2, 8, 11, 12)
Offering: (10:5, 8, 10, 14, 18)
Sacrifice: (8:3; 9:9, 23, 26; 10:1, 5, 8, 11, 12)
Covenant: (8:6, 8, 9, 10; 9:4, 15, 16, 17, 20; 10:16)
Blood: (9:7, 12, 13, 14, 18, 19, 20, 21, 22, 25; 10:4)
Sin: (8:12; 9:26, 28; 10:2, 3, 4, 5, 11, 12, 17, 18)

These and similar terms well illustrate the ceremonial vocabulary of the author and how he chooses to portray the greatest event in history—Christ's offering of himself.

Worship under the Old Covenant (9:1 – 10)

In chapter 8 the author has alluded to the two sanctuaries, the real one in heaven where Christ ministers and the other which is no more than its "copy and shadow." Chapter 9 contrasts these sanctuaries and especially the sacrifices that are offered in each.

Any reader with a Jewish background knew very well about the tabernacle. It had, of course, its "regulations for worship" (v. 1), which the author is about to describe. (Notice the word "regulations" appears again in verse 10, which closes the unit on old covenant worship.) But worship conducted in the tabernacle, and, by implication, that of the later temple, was inferior. It was, the author says, "earthly." It belonged to this world, in contrast with the heavenly sanctuary not made with hands (vv. 11, 24).

The earthly tabernacle consisted of two compartments. Because they were separated by a veil or curtain (Exod. 26:33), the author speaks of them as two distinct tents. The first compartment was called "the Holy Place." In it stood the seven-branched lampstand (see Exod. 25:31–10), the table (see Exod. 25:23–29), and the bread of the Presence (see Exod. 25:30; Lev. 24:5–9). The bread of Presence ("shewbread," KJV), if literally translated from the equivalent Hebrew term, means "bread of the face," that is, bread set out in the Presence of God.

The second compartment, the innermost behind the veil, was especially hallowed. It was the holiest of all places (literally, "the Holy of Holies"), and it could be entered only once a year (v. 7). The author goes on to say that the inner chamber contained "the golden altar of incense and the ark of the covenant" (v. 4).* According to Exodus 30:6 the altar of incense was placed "before the veil" in order that the incense burned on it could penetrate the veil and shroud the Divine Presence. Clearly, the altar and the ark were closely associated on the annual Day of Atonement (Exod. 30:10).

The "ark of the covenant" is described in more detail, since it was the most important article of furniture in the "Holy of Holies." It was covered with gold and included the golden jar with manna (see Exod. 16:31–36), Aaron's staff that miraculously sprouted (see Num. 17:1–10), and the two stone tablets of the covenant (see Deut. 10:1–5). Later, when the temple was built, the ark contained only the stone tablets (1 Kings 8:9).

Above the ark were two "cherubim of glory overshadowing the mercy seat" (v. 5). The cherubs were winged beings, usually thought of as sphinxlike in appearance. Their wings were spread out from each end of the lid of the ark, over the "mercy seat," the place of atonement.

*On the altar and its location, see my additional note in *Jesus Christ Today,* p. 178. Perhaps the author of Hebrews is here speaking quite generally, as someone might say, "My office has a secretary's office." This does not mean, of course, that the secretary's office is physically inside the other office. It means that the secretary's office in some way is connected or associated with the main office.

There God, symbolically, met with his people through his priestly representatives. There, on the solemn Day of Atonement, the high priest sprinkled the blood of the sacrificed bull and then of the goat for the people's sins (see Exod. 25:17–24; Lev. 16:2, 11–15).

But the author does not wish to speak of these things in more detail. He does not question that these old "regulations for worship" were given by God. Indeed, the tabernacle, earthly though it might be, was made strictly "according to the pattern." But the holiness of the tabernacle, the glittering gold of its furnishings, and such things, could not compare with the sacrifice of Christ!

This is what the author is anxious to prove. From our point of view, it is all so obvious. But for anyone born a Jew—even if he had become a Christian—it was not so simple. The author had to delineate how temporary and imperfect the old arrangements were when seen from the divine perspective.

As to their ritual services, the "Holy Place" and the "Holy of Holies" were quite distinct. They are contrasted in verses 6–7, which may be represented as follows:

"Holy Place"	"Holy of Holies"
outer tent	inner ("second") tent
priests	high priest only
go continually	once a year
ritual duties (trim lamps, incense, etc.)	blood (sprinkled for atonement)

To this sketch a few comments need to be added.

First, "continually" is the author's vivid touch in portraying the daily functions of the ordinary priests. Second, "once" is a significant term used characteristically to refer to Christ's sacrifice. The high priestly offering has its "once" also, but it was "once a year"—not "once and for all," as with Christ's offering of himself. Third, "not without blood" lays stress upon the inaccessibility of the "Holy of Holies." The high priest dare not enter, even once a year for a few moments, except with the blood of the bull and the goat (there were other precautions as well; read the entire chapter of Leviticus 16). Fourthly, "errors [literally, ignorances] of the people," denotes inadvertent sins, which were the only sins that could be atoned for (Num. 15:27–31). Something besides Moses' law was needed to deal with all kinds of sin! What was that to be?

In all of these rites the author sees the hand of God. The Holy Spirit provided for the law and its ordinances of worship. As long as the outer tent was standing, "the way into the sanctuary" was not yet opened (v. 8). It was the veil that separated the outer tent from the inner one, and it was the veil that was the perennial problem. It shut the people out and shut God in. Take away the veil, and immediately the way into God's presence is open.

The point is elaborated further: the outer tent was "symbolic [literally, a parable] for the present age" (v. 9). It was a parable in cloth, that the old externals were to last only "until the time of reformation" (v. 10). Yet no matter what the gifts and sacrifices were, they could not "perfect the conscience of the worshiper" (v. 9). No heap of sacrifices or legal ordinances could make the guilty conscience clean or bring the worshiper nearer to God.

So the whole ancient system was at fault. And what a futile system it was that could "deal only with food and drink and various ablutions [washings]" (v. 10). The Levitical law gave specific instructions on what to eat and what to drink. And there were so many prescribed washings— washings for the high priest, for the priests, for the Levites, for garments and vessels, and so forth. "Wash, wash, wash," the author is thinking, "and never, never made clean." Petty things, "regulations for the body," only temporary—"until the time of reformation"!

"The Heart of Hebrews" (9:11–14)

A few years ago, while working in the Manuscripts Room of the Cambridge University Library, I examined a little piece of papyrus with a few words of the Greek text of Hebrews written on it. I had studied other New Testament manuscripts, a number of them in various libraries at Cambridge (including even the famous Codex Bezae); but this was for me a memorable experience because the text of this Hebrews fragment is a portion of "the Heart of Hebrews."

It is certainly correct to speak of 9:11–14 as "the Heart of Hebrews." As to their location, these verses are right in the middle of the central section of Hebrews, 8:1–10:18. They are the central verses in the central section, the very center of the center. As to their structure, it is significant that the first word (in Greek) of these verses is "Christ." In all of Hebrews, this is the first and only time that "Christ" occurs at the beginning of a sentence and, importantly, also at the beginning of a new section. In chapter 8 and thus far in chapter 9, the author has made no direct reference to Christ. (Some translations insert "Christ" or "Jesus" in 8:6, but the Greek text simply reads "he.") The author holds any such reference in reserve, waiting, waiting. Then, at the precise moment all at once he declares, Christ appeared! As to their subject matter, these verses should be underscored in red. The last phrase of verse 10 is "until the time of reformation." The time of reformation was not the time of Martin Luther. Luther did a great work, but the true reformation was inaugurated by Christ. When Christ came, that was the greatest day in the history of the world. The author, however, is not thinking of the incarnation but of *Christ's entry into heaven as high priest*. He came as our high priest, and how different things have been ever since!

With Christ's coming, "good things" also "have come" to us (v. 11). The rest of verses 11–12 is complex and can be depicted as follows:

A. through the greater and more perfect tent
B. not made with hands . . . not of this creation
B. not through the blood of goats and calves
A. through his own blood
C. he entered once for all into the Holy Place . . . thus securing an eternal redemption

Notice the author's use of inverted order (ABBA pattern) and his climactic statement (C).

Let us try to picture in our minds the glorious scene the author is suggesting. The only Son has been away from home for long years. Obediently, he had gone to the cross. Now all heaven awaits his return, and what a day it must have been. "Lift up your heads, O gates! and be lifted up, O ancient doors! that the King of glory may come in. Who is the King of glory? The LORD, strong and mighty, the LORD, mighty in battle!" (Ps. 24:7–8).

When the Son enters heaven, what is the first thing he does? He goes in to the Father. (Understand that the whole scene is figurative.) And how does he enter before the Father? He passes through the greater, celestial tent, with his own blood. He sprinkles that blood on the heavenly mercy seat, in the very presence of God—and so he obtains for us not an annual but an eternal redemption. Figuratively speaking, Christ offers his blood in heaven, and he does it but once. He does not need to go in and out and in again because God says, "I will remember their sins no more."

The superiority of Christ's sacrifice is now defended by a "how much more" kind of argument. "For if the sprinkling of defiled persons with the blood of goats and bulls and with the ashes of a heifer sanctifies for the purification of the flesh, how much more shall the blood of Christ

. . . purify your conscience from dead works to serve the living God" (vv. 13–14).

From the Jewish viewpoint, the Levitical sacrifices were adequate enough for a person's ritual impurities. If, for example, someone touched a human bone or a dead body and became ceremonially unclean, he was to be sprinkled with "the ashes of a heifer" mixed with water (Numbers 19). But far worse than external uncleanness is sin within, for which little could be done by the goat and bull sacrificed on the Day of Atonement.

Or let us put the matter from our standpoint. Suppose you had to offer a sacrifice every time you committed a sin, every time you stormed out against a friend, or cut him down, every time you had just a touch of envy in your heart. Would you not always be offering sacrifices? Or take the opposite. Suppose, knowing all the time that you needed to, you did not make an hourly or daily offering. What then? What about your guilty conscience and your day-to-day relationship with God?

The answer is Christ's unblemished self-offering made through his own eternal Spirit. How very much more is the blood of Christ able to cleanse the nagging, hurting, sinful conscience!

> Guilty, vile and helpless we;
> Spotless Lamb of God was he;
> "Full atonement!" Can it be?
> Hallelujah! What a Savior!*

But the cleansed conscience is not an end in itself. It is for a set purpose, "so that we might serve [worship] the living God" (v. 14 NIV). "Serve" is the author's term for "serve in worship." Earlier he has described "the regulations for worship" (v. 1; cf. v. 10) and the priests in their

---

*Philip P. Bliss, "Hallelujah! What a Savior," hymn.

"ritual duties" (literally, "worship duties," v. 6). He now concludes his grand section on Christ's priestly offering with the thought that we, who are wondrously purified within, are to give ourselves in dedicated service/worship to the true God.

Christ's Sacrifice and the New Covenant (9:15—22)

We have now arrived at a point where we can treat more briefly the rest of chapter 9. With his consummate presentation of Christ's entry into heaven by means of his own blood, the author now enlarges upon the necessity of Christ's death.

1. Christ's death inaugurated the new covenant foretold in Jeremiah 31. Of this covenant he is both inaugurator (or "mediator," 8:6) and guarantor (7:22).

2. Christ's death redeemed the sins of those who lived under the first covenant. If animal sacrifices were wholly unable to deal with sin, what about all those who died under Moses' law? "Do you mean to say," the Jews would ask, "that our forefathers perished without hope?"

The answer is an emphatic "No!" The people who lived under the old covenant did not have to pay the price of their sins. The sacrifice of Christ did that for them. Christ "redeemed" them, which means not that he bought them back (the original idea of "redeem"), but that he "liberated" them and set them free from their sins (cf. 2:15).

3. Christ's death makes it possible that those "who are called may receive the promised eternal inheritance" (v. 15). Christians, specifically, have been called through the preaching of the gospel (cf. 3:1). But Christ died for all. His blood reaches both directions, for those under both covenants. So the promised inheritance, which is "eternal" (cf. 9:12, 14), is for all of God's people—if only they remain faithful.

Christ's death was absolutely necessary, especially so for the reception of the inheritance. The author illustrates. In the case of a will, the person who makes the will, the testator, must die. In making his point, the author uses one word (Greek, *diatheke*) in two senses, both for "covenant" and for "will." Christ is both mediator and testator. As testator he had to die in order to convey to us the inheritance of salvation.

"Even the first covenant was not ratified without blood" (v. 18). The connection with the foregoing is not obvious, but the author simply wants to show that whether we speak of "will" or "covenant," death has to occur. That is, Christ had to die. When the old covenant was inaugurated, Moses took the blood of the sacrificed animals and sprinkled it on the people (Exod. 24:3–8). The author says also that the book of the covenant was sprinkled, a detail not mentioned in Exodus but probable if almost all things were cleansed by blood (v. 22).

The summary statements on blood reinforce the main point on Christ's death. Under the law almost everything was "purified with blood" (for exceptions, see Num. 31:21–24; Lev. 5:11–13). "And without the shedding of blood there is no forgiveness" (v. 22). The latter statement is practically a proverb, based on Leviticus 17:11, that "it is the blood that makes atonement." Thus the author's emphasis in this chapter can be seen in three similar maxims:

not without blood (v. 7)
not ratified without blood (v. 18)
not without the shedding of blood (v. 22)

The Finality of Christ's Sacrifice (9:23–28)

The concluding verses of chapter 9 look back and direct attention to the important central section, especially

9:11–12. Once again we are at "the Heart of Hebrews," where Christ is depicted as making his triumphant entry into heaven as our high priest.

Resuming his previous thought the author reasons that if the "copies of the heavenly things" (the tabernacle, etc.; cf. 8:5) needed purification with animal blood, "the heavenly things themselves [required] . . . better sacrifices" (v. 23). The language is figurative. The author is not saying that heaven had to be cleansed of Satan or evil or whatever. He speaks figuratively and comparatively. If earthly things had to be purged with sacrifices, the heavenly things had to be cleansed as well. But what could cleanse heaven? Only "better sacrifices"—the sacrifice of Christ offered in heaven.

The next statement makes this even clearer: "For Christ has entered, not into a sanctuary made with hands . . . but into heaven itself, now to appear in the presence of God on our behalf" (v. 24). This is one of the very great verses of Hebrews, echoing the great verses in 9:11–12. Christ as our high priest did not go into some sacred room inside some earthly temple. He went into heaven itself, into the very presence of God. Did you ever read of the Jewish high priest's entering in to make atonement and staying in the divine presence? But Christ is *now* there *for us!* ("Now . . . for us" are emphatic in the Greek sentence.) Now after long centuries, when the earthly Holy of Holies had no one to represent the people, except for a few moments a year, Christ has entered heaven and so always represents us before God.

Nor did Christ have to offer himself "repeatedly . . . for then he would have had to suffer repeatedly since the foundation of the world" (vv. 25–26). "Repeatedly" indicates imperfection and futility. Christ's offering was so fully satisfactory, he never needs to do it again. Truly, it was "once and for all" (7:27; 9:12). And *when* Christ appeared is significant. "At the climax of history" (REB), he came "to put away sin by the sacrifice of himself" (v. 26).

A further point on the one-time sacrifice of Christ is made by way of illustration. "Just as it is appointed for men to die once, and after that comes judgment, so Christ having been offered once . . . will appear a second time" (vv. 27–28). The meaning is not that we as human beings are "appointed" to die, or that as individuals each one has his or her predetermined hour for death. Instead, the thought is that as men die only once, so Christ died only once "to bear the sins of many" (cf. 2:9–10).

And Christ "will appear a second time." He will have to leave the heavenly sanctuary, but never again will he have to atone for sin. Rather, when he comes again, it will be "to save those who are eagerly waiting for him."

Remember earlier, in a key verse, Christ was announced as "the source of eternal salvation to all who obey him" (5:9). For several chapters, this has been the substance of the author's message. Christ is the fountainhead, the giver, the cause of eternal salvation. In his first appearance, because of his exquisite offering, he is Christ the Savior. When he comes a second time for those who keenly await him, again he will be Christ the Savior. "Beautiful Savior!"

QUESTIONS

1. Why does the author of Hebrews begin chapter 9 with a description of the earthly tabernacle? What does he say about the "regulations for worship" associated with the tabernacle?
2. What is "the time of reformation" (9:10)? How is this contrasted with matters of "food and drink"?
3. Discuss and explain 9:11–14 as "the Heart of Hebrews." Describe Christ's entry into the heavenly "Holy Place" and the offering of his blood in heaven.

4. How does the offering of Christ's blood affect *your* conscience and *your* worship?
5. On what basis were transgressions forgiven under the old covenant (9:15)? How is our situation different from theirs?
6. What does the author mean by "better sacrifices" (9:23)? Why does he use such language?
7. True or False. Christ must come again to deal with sin for one last time.

10

Jesus, the Better Sacrifice: Part 2

Hebrews 10:1—18

. . . the heavenly things themselves with better sacrifices . . .

HEBREWS 9:23

Hebrews 9:1–10:18 concludes the author's argument that Christ is the one and only high priest for believers. The focus of this grand section is on Christ's priestly service in heaven and the metaphorical offering of his blood before the Father in the heavenly Holy of Holies. For convenience' sake, we have divided this section into two parts.

The opening verses of chapter 10 appear at first glance to be repetitious, but they lead into the important point of Christ's voluntary submission to do God's true will on sacrifice. If apart from sacrificial blood, there is no forgiveness (9:22), and if it is impossible for animal blood to afford that forgiveness (10:4), then it follows that Christ's offering of himself is the only remedy for sin.

Shadow and Reality (10:1–4)

The ineffectiveness of the entire Levitical ritual is laid down once again. The law was no more than a "shadow of the good things to come." "The good things" are especially the "better sacrifices" presented by the heavenly high priest; and because they have been offered for our sins, the good things for us have already arrived (9:11). The law was a "shadow." Think of it as both "shadow" and "foreshadow," for the author uses now one and then the other aspect of the term. The sacrifices of the law were no more than a dim outline (cf. 8:5), but they looked ahead and "foreshadowed" the real sacrifice of Christ.

But the Levitical sacrifices, in their ceaseless repetition, could never "make perfect" the former worshipers. They attempted to draw near to God through their sacrifices, but the law perfected no one (7:19, 12). "If the worshipers had once been cleansed, they would no longer have any consciousness of sin" (v. 2; cf. 9:9). Always their consciences haunted them. Always there was the unsettled score of their offenses.

We might think that the annual Day of Atonement would extend a measure of relief from sin's guilt. Actually, the opposite was true. It was the one day during the year when every Jew was required to fast, and it was the one day when the whole nation confessed its sins (Lev. 16:20–22, 29–31). All the day's activities were designed to emphasize the enormity of sin. "In these sacrifices there is a reminder of sin year after year" (v. 3).

It is interesting to notice that the noun "reminder" ("remembrance") occurs in the New Testament only here and in accounts of the Lord's Supper (Luke 22:19; 1 Cor. 11:24–25). This may be only incidental, but one cannot help but think of the contrast suggested. In the old covenant there was a yearly "remembrance" of sin. In the new covenant there is a weekly "remembrance" of him who has effectively dealt with sin.

The author now caps his fundamental point: "It is impossible that the blood of bulls and goats should take away sins" (v. 4). Well, that should settle the whole matter! Who would want to return to a system so empty and so futile? It is self-evident that animal sacrifices cannot remove the guilt of human sin.

We are ready to ask, why did God command these sacrifices to be offered? The immediate answer is that God wanted the person to feel some responsibility for his actions and that he ought to do something or offer something for his sins. On the other hand, there are several other factors that we should not overlook.

1. Moses' law, as we have already learned, did not make provisions for all kinds of sins (Num. 15:27–31).

2. Christ's death, as we have seen, reaches back in its effects to all those who lived under the first covenant (9:15).

3. Even under the first covenant, many of the prophets taught that God expected more of his people than the offerings of blood and flesh. We will notice below some of the Old Testament passages that make this crystal clear.

4. The Pentateuchal laws, by what they could not cover, call attention to their own inadequacy and so indirectly point to Christ.

The Perfect Sacrifice (10:5—10)

In this section we enter into a beautiful passage found in Psalm 40:6–8. The words quoted give us a kind of conversation between the eternal Son and God the Father, with the Son as the speaker. Because the Levitical sacrifices were so totally ineffective, Christ resolves to come into the created world and perfectly fulfill God's will on sacrifice.

The words of the psalm read: "Sacrifices and offerings thou has not desired, but a body hast thou prepared for me; in burnt offerings and sin offerings thou hast taken no pleasure. Then I said, 'Lo, I have come to do thy will, O God'" (vv. 6–7).

A number of Old Testament passages say that even a host of sacrifices given to God is not enough:

> I will accept no bull from your house, nor he-goat from your folds. Do I eat the flesh of bulls, or drink the blood of goats? (Ps. 50:9, 13)

> For thou hast no delight in sacrifice; were I to give a burnt offering thou wouldst not be pleased. (Ps. 51:16)

> What to me is the multitude of your sacrifices? says the Lord; I have had enough of burnt offerings of rams, and the fat of fed beasts; I do not delight in the blood of bulls, or of lambs, or of he-goats. (Isa. 1:11; cf. Jer. 7:21–22; Amos 5:21–23; Micah 6:6–7)

When read in their full contexts, these passages make it clear that sacrifices made to God must be accompanied with a true spirit of obedience:

> Offer to God a sacrifice of thanksgiving. (Ps. 50:14)

> The sacrifice acceptable to God is a broken spirit. (Ps. 51:17)

> I delight to do thy will, O my God; thy law is within my heart. (Ps. 40:8)

Psalm 40 is a classic statement of this principle. The coming Messiah, who knows the mind of God, knows the will of God. Burnt offerings and sin offerings could not atone. So the Son declares that he will accomplish God's perfect will by use of a "body" provided for him.

Originally, the psalmist spoke these words of himself, having read about obedience in the scroll-book of God's law. But the author sees a far deeper meaning stored up in the lines. To him they refer to none other than Jesus who, through all his days on earth, supremely obeyed God. "Not my will but thy will be done" was in his heart, written of him, figuratively speaking, in the scroll-book.

So Christ became incarnate to take care of an ineffective sacrificial structure and to displace it with an entirely new one—the free, loving sacrifice of himself. Consequently—and here the author uses forceful language to accentuate his point—"He abolishes the first in order to establish the second" (v. 9). The word "abolish" ordinarily refers to a "violent killing." It is used of the "massacre" of the baby boys in Bethlehem (Matt. 2:15), of Jesus' execution (Luke 23:32; Acts 10:39), and of his final "destruction" of the lawless one with "the breath of his mouth" (2 Thess. 2:8). The point here is that Christ has once and for all "annihilated" the Levitical system of sacrifice.

Thus, the complete fulfillment of God's will, referred to in the psalm, is the perfect obedience of Christ. Indeed, "will" here has two aspects. From one standpoint, it is the will of God that Christ came to do. From the other, it is the will of Christ himself. And the two wills merge perfectly into one in Christ's perfect obedience to God.

It is by that will, the author says, that "we have been sanctified through the offering of the body of Jesus once for all" (v. 10). "Sanctification," as we have seen, denotes a ritual cleansing that enables one to approach God in worship. Jesus went to the cross for us, and God forgave sin. "Once for all," placed at the end of the sentence, stresses again the finality of Jesus' sacrifice.

Seated at God's Right Hand (10:11–18)

We now draw to the end of the great, central section. The sacrifice of Christ, once made, ever lives on in its effects. The author underscores this by setting a vivid contrast before us.

"Every [Jewish] priest stands daily at his service, offering repeatedly the same sacrifices, which can never take away sins" (v. 11; cf. v. 1). Each word adds impact. "Every" recalls the many priests over the years. There they were in their regular course, "daily" offering their same old sacrifices. And there they *stood*, every single one of them. Remember that in the earthly tabernacle one item of furniture was noticeably absent—a seat. There was no seat for the priest, no throne for the high priest. (Oh, how a good high priest must have longed to go into the inner Holy of Holies and sit for a while in the presence of God!) But the priests had to perform many ceremonies, and there was no place for them to sit. And they were always offering the same old things, with the same vain results.

All this is contrasted with the great Priest-King on the divine throne. "But when Christ had offered for all time a single sacrifice for sins, he sat down at the right hand of God" (v. 12). The language, as we have seen throughout, is expressed in exquisite figures. God literally has no right hand; Christ literally does not sit in heaven. Figuratively and ceremonially, Christ sits next to God, and his sitting demonstrates the completion of his atoning work. As a priest he had something to offer (8:3). What a magnificent offering it was!

He who humbled himself on earth is now exalted in heaven, waiting, as Psalm 110:1 says, "until his enemies should be made a stool for his feet" (v. 13). That is complete victory for him, and utter subjection for his enemies. Why? The truth, already made unforgettable, is stated one more time: "For by a single offering he has perfected for all time those who are sanctified" (v. 14).

Recall that in Hebrews 8 the author introduced the oracle of Jeremiah 31, proving that centuries before Christ came God envisioned a new covenant for his people. The old covenant had to give way to a new, better covenant inscribed on the heart. Here the author picks up the lines of Jeremiah again, but now with a special touch. The Holy Spirit in Scripture, he says, "bears witness to us; for after saying, 'This is the covenant that I will make' . . . then he adds, 'I will remember their sins and their misdeeds no more'" (vv. 15–17).

Why does the author now restate this line from Jeremiah? Because it focuses on the promises (8:6) of the new covenant which, above all, make the new covenant better. On an earthly cross, Christ offered himself for sin and willingly completed the will of God on sacrifice. God in his grace established that standard of sacrifice, and in his grace he fully accepted it. If that be the case, the author assures us "where there is forgiveness . . . there is no longer any offering for sin" (v. 18).

Thus, the grand, central section (8:1–10:18) closes on the highest note and affirmation of Hebrews, that forgiveness of sins, truly and fully and finally, has been secured for us by our great high priest. The old sacrificial system made nothing perfect (7:19); it could not bring about a right relationship with God. Why not? Because it had no ultimate ground or basis for it. Of all things, *the old covenant lacked Christ*—the only "source of eternal salvation" (5:9).

The author has taken great pains to establish this. It is the heart and soul of his message. Indeed, it is the message of the gospel; and it is significant not only how Hebrews contributes to this message but that it teaches in its own way the same gospel proclaimed by Christ's apostles. How regrettable that the modern mind often hears Hebrews with heavy ears and contents itself with subtle substitutes!

In summary, the author has placed before us, with consummate skill, Jesus as our eternal high priest. As priest, especially when compared with the candidates from Levi, he has no rivals. He exemplifies the perfect type of priesthood, what God had in mind from the beginning. And he is the very kind of priest all of us need. No shadows here! He is the *real* thing!

1. His incarnation was *real*. He descended to earth and fully shared in flesh and blood. He was not ashamed of his "brothers." In every respect he had to be made like them (2:11–17).

2. His suffering was *real*. As the author will go on to say, he "suffered outside the gate" (13:12). He "endured the cross" (12:2). He was made "perfect through suffering" (2:10). Son though he was, he "learned" obedience though his suffering (5:8).

3. His offering was made in the *real* place—heaven itself. The difference between an "earthly sanctuary" (9:1), the tabernacle, where the Jewish high priest officiated, and the sanctuary "not made with hands" (9:11), where Christ ministers, is infinite. As high priest for us, Christ gloriously entered heaven. What could he offer? Certainly not the blood of bulls and goats! Through his own eternal spirit and through his own blood, he went before God. There he sprinkled his blood on the mercy seat in heaven.

4. His forgiveness is *real*. This, of course, follows, if Christ's offering of his blood before the Father has secured "eternal redemption" (9:12). An ancient king customarily had a special attendant to remind him of this or that which had occurred in the past. The attendant kept notes and chronicles in case something had to be recalled. He was a "remembrancer." But because of Christ, we do not

have a "remembrancer" to bring up our offenses. God has said, "I will remember their sins no more."

So it is Christ who turns shadows to reality. His blood can really deal with a sin-submerged conscience. His blood can wash away our sins. Instead of "woe is me, woe is me, woe is me," with confidence and great joy, we can say, "thank God, thank God, thank God" for Jesus Christ. "Hallelujah! What a Savior!"

QUESTIONS

1. Explain how the law was "a shadow of the good things to come" (10:1). How was the Day of Atonement a "reminder of sin" (10:3)?

2. Discuss the significance of the statement that "it was impossible for the blood of bulls and goats to take away sins" (10:4).

3. How do the words of Psalm 40:6–8 fit the sacrifice of Christ?

4. Hebrews 10:10 is a key verse. Explain these terms: "will," "sanctified," "offering," "body," and "once for all."

5. Hebrews 10:11–18 is the author's summary of the grand middle section (8:1–10:18). What are the chief points of this summary? Can you parallel these with some of the author's previous statements?

6. "It is Christ who turns shadows to reality." Comment on this.

11

A Call to Draw Near

Hebrews 10:19—39

Let us draw near with a true heart.
HEBREWS 10:22

Let us take a moment to review the logical arrangement of these middle chapters of Hebrews.

5:11–6:20   Exhortation: on to mature teaching
7:1–28   Christ, like Melchizedek
8:1–10:18   Christ, source of eternal salvation
10:19–39   Exhortation: a call to draw near

Look how balanced the structure is and how it focuses on Christ.

The author has now completed his crowning exposition of Christ as "the source of eternal salvation" (cf. 5:9). As our high priest, Christ had something to offer:

himself. His blood, so selflessly and willingly offered, is God's final remedy for a disturbed conscience.

Confidence to Draw Near (10:19—25)

With 10:19 we come to a high point of exhortation. Actually, the remainder of Hebrews is a remarkable intermingling of exhortation and warning.

Christians have been set free from their guilty consciences in order that they might "serve [worship] the living God" (9:14). Now the author implores his readers to do this very thing. Why not, he says, just go right on into God's presence and offer him grateful worship? The author's appeal begins, "Therefore, brethren, since we have confidence to enter the sanctuary by the blood of Jesus." "The sanctuary" is the heavenly one; and all of us are encouraged to enter it. The point is that, though we still live by faith (v. 23), the veil has been removed, and we can now with full freedom enter where God is. To be sure, this is not of our own merit but is wholly due to the atoning blood of Jesus, our Beautiful Savior and High Priest.

This way to God is further described as "new" and "living." It is "new" because it was only recently made available. It is "living" because it is "life-giving," the way that leads to eternal life. This way, the author goes on to state, was opened up by Christ, "through the curtain, that is, through his flesh" (v. 20). "The curtain," or veil, stood between man and God. Figuratively speaking, the author calls it Christ's flesh. That is, his fleshly death, like the veil, stood between him and his entrance before God. This clearly is what the author means as seen by the parallel expressions which describe how divine access was secured:

By the blood of Jesus. (v. 19)
Through his flesh. (v. 20)

And since, the author adds, "we have a great priest over the house of God, let us draw near with a true heart in full assurance of faith" (vv. 21–22; cf. 4:14; 3:6). By "draw near" the author means that we should "draw near to God" (as in 10:1; cf. 7:25; 11:6). The similar exhortation in 4:16 is for us to come near to the God of grace in prayer. Here the exhortation refers more generally to all aspects of worship. Notice, we meet again the "let us" kind of exhortation:

> Let us draw near . . . in . . . faith. (v. 22)
> Let us hold fast . . . our hope. (v. 23)
> Let us . . . stir up . . . to love. (v. 24)

Faith, hope, and love are foundation stones for Christian living. These await their further development in chapters 11–13.

Our approach/worship to God must be made with "a true heart." It is not to be like the Levitical priest who came before God externally perfect but with a dead heart. It is to be an entrance of sincerity, "in full assurance of faith" (cf. 6:11)—without any doubt or hesitation whatever.

The privilege of approaching God in worship assumes that certain conditions have been met. We have already had "our hearts sprinkled clean from an evil conscience and our bodies washed with pure water" (v. 22). This means that, figuratively speaking, our hearts have been sprinkled with the blood of Christ, and so our guilty consciences have been relieved (cf. 9:14). That we have been "washed" refers back to our baptism (cf. Acts 22:16). Paul uses similar language: "you were washed, you were sanctified, you were justified in the name of the Lord Jesus Christ and in the Spirit of our God" (1 Cor. 6:10; cf. Eph. 5:26; Titus 3:5).

The exhortation continues. "Let us hold fast the confession of our hope without wavering, for he who promised is faithful" (v. 23). Previously, the author has urged his readers along these lines, that they "hold fast" to

Christ no matter what the obstacles might be (3:6, 14; 4:14). "Hope" here refers to what we hope for, as in 6:18, where we are "to seize" the hope that is in front of us. The basis of our hope is directly related to Christ's priestly entrance into the heavenly sanctuary (cf. 6:19) and to God's promise that can never prove false (cf. 6:18).

To faith and hope the author adds love. "Let us consider how to stir up one another to love and good works" (v. 24). The thought in Greek is not "consider how" but "consider one another" to spur on to love and practical goodness. Love does not just happen, nor do good works.

What we all need is mutual love and mutual incitement. This is, or certainly should be, available in the public assembly. The next verse says, "Not neglecting to meet together . . . but encouraging one another" (v. 25). Why should we gather together? Because we, like the first readers, need exhortation, and because we need actively to encourage others in the assembly. And by encouraging one another, we join hands with the author who is writing this letter as a "word of exhortation" (13:22; cf. 3:13).

Persecuted Christians especially must have such encouragement. Sadly, some of them had dropped out from the very thing they needed. And mutual edification was necessary all the more since "the Day [was] drawing near." "Day" is the last word in the Greek sentence and so receives special emphasis. The day that approached them is "the day of the Lord," the day of God's final judgment. Notice how this last clause in verse 25 is connected with the next paragraph. "For if we willfully persist in sin" (v. 26 NRSV), what is there for us? Only a "fearful prospect of judgment" (v. 27).

Another Warning against Apostasy (10:26–31)

Reference to "the Day" leads to a further warning concerning unbelief and apostasy (cf. 3:12). "For if we sin deliberately after receiving the knowledge of the truth, there no longer remains a sacrifice for sins" (v. 26). Thus begin the severe tones of a passage similar to 6:4–8. There, as here, the danger is of a complete falling away from the faith. The author is not referring to ordinary sins of human weakness and temptation. Earlier he has assured us that Christ deeply "feels with" our failings and "bears gently" with us when we go astray (4:15; 5:2).

By contrast, the author is speaking of that sort of sin described in Numbers 15:30 when a person commits sin "with a high hand." What does this mean? The passage goes on to explain. That person "reviles the Lord" and "shall be cut off from among the people . . . his iniquity shall be upon him" (Num. 15:30–31). The meaning of "cut off" is shown in the next paragraph, where God commands a man to be stoned who gathered sticks on the Sabbath (vv. 32–36).

"Deliberately" is the first word of the Greek sentence in verse 26, laying stress on the defiant nature of the sin described. What the author has in mind is a deliberate rejection of truth after truth has been once received, a snuffing out of light that once shone in the heart, a choosing of the dark with open eyes. He speaks not so much of an act of sin but of a state of sin—"if we go on sinning deliberately." Whoever would do this, as Numbers says, "his iniquity shall be upon him." If a person abandons Christ and rejects his covenant, where can he go for forgiveness? To the blood of bulls and goats? No! This is precisely the point. If one dares to reject Christ, he has no place to turn. He has spurned his only hope!

If sin bears its consequences, then surely knowingly and willfully persisting in sin can lead to "a fearful prospect of judgment" (v. 27). This is the same kind of judgment which awaits God's enemies, "a fury of fire" that will "consume the adversaries."

God's fierce anger against apostates is accented by reference to the law of Moses. According to Deuteronomy 17:2–7, a man or woman guilty of idolatry was to die "without mercy" on the evidence of "two or three witnesses." If that was true under Moses' law, the author reasons, "how much worse punishment" will be deserved by the person who, after receiving the truth, flatly rejects the blessings of Christ's saving work?

Clearly, the whole passage concerns blatant rebellion and apostasy. The author proceeds to define the person "who goes on sinning deliberately." The apostate (1) "has spurned the Son of God." To "spurn" means to "trample underfoot," just as salt paths are stamped down by continual walking (cf. Matt. 5:13). Treading underfoot "the Son of God" suggests not merely a denial but a personal affront to him.

The apostate (2) has "profaned the blood of the covenant by which he was sanctified." This, of course, refers to the atoning blood of Christ, the blood that established the new covenant (9:15–22; 13:20). On one hand, the apostate looks on the blood of Christ as no different from anyone else's, and, on the other hand, regards his covenant as invalid and meaningless. The irony is that the apostate counts Christ's blood as "unholy," the very blood which once had made him holy.

The apostate (3) has "outraged the Spirit of grace." The apostate, who holds Christ in contempt, likewise insults the Holy Spirit through whom God's saving grace has come. How unimaginable that former Christians could ever act like this! But hardened hearts that persist in sin can grow bitter. Here they have turned on Christ and have become his inveterate enemies. Readers, then and now, must take heed.

Indeed, God's judgment on his adversaries is inevitable. God speaks in Scripture and declares, "'Vengeance is mine, I will repay.' And again, 'The Lord will judge his people.'" The quotations, from the Song of Moses in Deuteronomy (32:35–36), were well known to Jewish people and are made for maximum effect.

The somber passage comes to a close with one last warning: "It is a fearful thing to fall into the hands of the living God" (v. 31). The sentence is short, the point is sharp. "Fearful" is the first word in the Greek sentence. Notice, "fearful prospect of judgment" (v. 27), and "fearful" to fall into the avenging hands of God. Make no mistake. Divine punishment is sure for apostates.

But let us remember that things are vastly different for those who steadfastly rely on God. David in full trust said: "Let us fall into the hand of the LORD, for his mercy is great" (2 Sam. 24:14). For believers no hands are as gentle as God's hands.

Exhortation to Endurance (10:32—39)

Oh, what a gruesome picture of the end of apostates! Will the readers fall back and fall away, or will they continue in the Christian way? The author's call for them, here and in the remainder of the letter, is a call for a spirit of heroic endurance.

Indeed, this is the way they had started out. "Recall the former days," he says, when "you endured a hard struggle with sufferings" (v. 32). Exactly when this was, we do not know.

It is clear, however, that shortly after the readers' conversions, after they had been "enlightened" with the new light of Christ, a period of persecution had set in. They had stood courageously. They had suffered much. Sometimes they were "publicly exposed to abuse and affliction."

At other times they were "partners with" those who were mistreated.

Not only so, but they had "had compassion on the prisoners" and had "joyfully accepted the plundering of [their] property" (v. 34). They had visited and given food to their fellows in prison—a sacred Christian responsibility (13:3; Matt. 25:31–46). Because they were Christians, their belongings had been wrenched from them, probably by a looting mob. Yet in these trials, they had rejoiced, just as Jesus had taught (Matt. 5:12) and his apostles had done (Acts 5:41). Their treasure was in heaven. They knew they "had a better possession and an abiding one."

Having reminded them of their glorious past, the author now pleads with them. "Therefore do not throw away your confidence, which has a great reward" (v. 35). "Throw away" is the opposite of "hold fast" (10:23; cf. 3:6, 14). The point is that they had endured so much, why should they now give up? "Confidence" refers to the believer's right to enter with assurance before God based on the sacrifice of Christ (4:16; 10:19), but it is also the term for "fearlessness" and "courage." Because of that assurance, Christians can have courage on the field of battle.

Indispensable for the critical hour is forward-pressing endeavor: "You have need of endurance, so that you may do the will of God and receive what is promised" (v. 36). Moses held on, as seeing the God who is invisible (11:27). Jesus endured the humiliation of the cross (12:2). So you, too, the author says to his readers, must endure. Endure what? Endure in doing God's will, even if it means suffering (cf. 1 Peter 4:19). The exhortation is similar to that of chapter 4: Cling tenaciously to your faith; make every effort to gain the promised inheritance.

But when would the inheritance be theirs? According to heaven's timetable, the fulfillment of the promise would soon take place. "For yet a little while, and the coming one shall come and shall not tarry" (v. 37). The quotation, which continues into the next verse, combines Isaiah 26:20 (LXX) and Habakkuk 2:3–4. Early Christians, troubled and tested, quite naturally would cry out and wonder if deliverance would ever come. The author responds that they need to wait only a little while, and then "the coming one" (the Messiah) would decisively appear.

The quotation from Habakkuk continues: "But my righteous one shall live by faith, and if he shrinks back, my soul has no pleasure in him" (v. 38). If you have read Romans and Galatians, you know these lines. Paul quotes this passage with a special emphasis, that the one grand principle which puts a person right with God is faith in Jesus Christ (see Rom. 1:17; 5:1; Gal. 3:11; 2:16).

But the word "faith" often has the sense of "faithfulness." This is its meaning here. The ancient prophet took his complaint to God, asking how long he would allow his people to be oppressed by their enemies. God's answer is that he is supreme and that he will bring down the wicked in due time. Meanwhile, the righteous shall live by their faithfulness.

Habakkuk and Hebrews present similar conditions. On one hand, the prophet cries, how long? On the other, harassed Christians seem perplexed over why the Lord has delayed his coming. If in Habakkuk the vision was sure to come, so in Hebrews the "coming one" will come and will not linger. And if in Habakkuk's time the righteous were to be saved by faithfully holding to God, faithfulness and endurance are required even more by the righteous addressed in this letter.

One further word of encouragement brings the chapter to an end. "We are not of those who shrink back and are destroyed, but of those who have faith and keep their souls" (v. 39). Notice that the author, again, seizes on key words in his Old Testament quotation. Placing himself with the readers, the author confidently says that "we" are not among those who "shrink back." "We," underlined, are not cowards but are people of "faith" who win their souls.

Plainly, there are only two alternatives before us. Either we hold on to God in faith, or we withdraw to apostasy and perish. What will it be? God indeed will do his part and more. But we must decide whether we want to be saved at the last, whether we will possess our souls, whether we will gain our lives through firm endurance (cf. Luke 21:19). May God give us strength that we may imitate those who through steadfast faith inherit the promises (6:12).

QUESTIONS

1. Compare 10:19 and 4:16. Why does 10:19 include "the blood of Jesus"? After reading 8:1–10:18, should we feel more confident to approach God?
2. How is the way into the heavenly sanctuary "new" and "living"? What does it mean to "draw near with a true heart" (10:22)?
3. Discuss and keep in mind each one of the "let us" expressions in verses 22–24.
4. Since we all need love and mutual encouragement, where especially, according to 10:25, should this take place?
5. How is the warning against deliberately continuing to sin (10:26) connected with the previous verse? Of whom is it said, "It is a fearful thing to fall into the hands of the living God" (10:31)?
6. What does 10:32–34 tell us about the readers' past experiences of persecution? Now, what do they need?

12

A Call to Faith

Hebrews 11:1 — 40

All these [were] well attested by their faith.
HEBREWS 11:39

We have now reached one of the truly outstanding chapters of the Bible, the great and wonderful chapter 11 on faith.

I have often asked students in my classes, "Why did Paul write the Corinthians an entire chapter on the resurrection (1 Cor. 15), and why did he write them the marvelous chapter on love (1 Cor. 13)?" Because they were the ones who needed these instructions! And why did the Hebrews author write his chapter on faith? Because his readers needed it! We may well read the love chapter or the faith chapter at special times, perhaps in some time of personal crisis. But we must remember that though they are beautiful in themselves, yet they are part and parcel of letters which have a first-century setting and meaning.

So as we read this great chapter, we must pay attention to its connections. At the end of chapter 10, two lines especially stand out: "You have need of endurance" (v. 36) and "we are . . . of those who have faith [faithfulness]" (v. 39). At the beginning of chapter 12, the exhortation is "Let us run with perseverance [endurance] the race that is set before us" (v. 1). Endurance and faith, then, are the key ideas that bracket chapter 11. Faith endures. In the midst of trials and chains and even torture, faith journeys on and waits for God to accomplish his promises.

You will recall that the author characteristically states beforehand the theme that he is about to pursue. We have called this an "announcement theme." Now we have arrived at the fourth of these announcement themes, PEOPLE OF FAITH (10:39), the theme which is to be developed through 12:11.

Introduction (11:1—2)

The author begins not so much with a definition of what faith is but with what faith does. How does faith act when God speaks? What does it mean to live by faith?

First, faith lives in confidence of the future. "Faith is the assurance of things hoped for" (v. 1; cf. 10:22–23). Faith always looks forward. It is remarkable how many times and in how many ways this is said. Abraham "looked forward to the city which has foundations" (v. 10). Moses "looked to the reward" (v. 26). People of faith are pilgrims who are "seeking a homeland" (v. 14). They long for "a better country" (v. 16; cf. vv. 13, 20–22, 33, 35).

Second, faith is living proof of the invisible. It is "the conviction [proof] of things not seen." Faith takes long views. It stakes itself on the reality of the unseen and is controlled by that reality. It can move courageously into the unknown because it sees "him who is invisible" (v. 27).

Living by faith, "the men of old received divine approval" (v. 2). The "men of old" ("elders" KJV) are those who are famous for their faith, of whom the author is about to speak. They, on the basis of their faith, won God's approval and are immortalized in Scripture.

Faith from the Beginning (11:3—7)

When teaching this material, I have often asked students to think of this chapter as pictures in a great art gallery. Most of the paintings on the walls are portraits, though some are of historical events. At the base of each painting is a title, *By Faith Noah*, *By Faith Abraham*, *By Faith Moses*, and so forth. What is the name of this gallery? Over the door is a sign that reads, "Heroes and Heroines of Faith."

Now let us go into the gallery and examine its paintings. The first thing we see is a picture of the universe in the first blush of creation. The author explains: "By faith we understand that the world was created by the word of God" (v. 3). Today many scientists theorize that the universe began with a "big bang." If we ask where the big bang came from, of course, science cannot explain. But suppose we had been there in the very beginning, looking over the Creator's shoulder. Would we really be much better off? Faith allows us to understand that everything we see came from what we cannot see.

The next painting is of Abel. He is offering a sacrifice. The author declares that his sacrifice was "more acceptable" than that of his brother Cain. Because of his faith, Abel received God's approval that he was "righteous"—righteous in the sense that he did the will of God. Abel died as the first of all martyrs, but his example of faith lives on.

After Abel comes Enoch's portrait. "Enoch walked [lived] with God; and he was not, for God took him" (Gen. 5:24). The LXX (the Septuagint, or Greek Old Testament) says that God "translated" Enoch. He did not die like others but was removed from earth to heaven. Walking or living with God, he walked home with him.

Instead of Enoch "walked with God," the LXX renders this more generally as Enoch "pleased God." The expression is especially significant for the author. He is sure that if Enoch "pleased" God, this can only mean that he had faith. So the author goes on to state that "without faith it is impossible to please [God]" (v. 6). Faith seeks God, as Enoch did; and faith receives a rich reward, just as Enoch did.

The forward-looking faith of Noah stands out, and we now come to him. What is he doing? He is building a ship on dry land! Why? Because God has warned him of an impending flood, of "events as yet unseen" (v. 7). Just as Jesus prayed with "reverent submission" (5:7 NRSV; Greek, *eulabeia*), so Noah "took reverent heed" (*eulabeomai*) and obeyed God by constructing an ark. Faith acts. Faith submits to God and obeys.

And when faith obeys God, it cannot help but condemn those who do not. It is in this sense that Noah "condemned the world" about him. He, listening to God's voice, entered the ark with his family. By his action he condemned the people around him. "The flood came and destroyed them all" (Luke 17:27).

The Faith of the Patriarchs (11:8 – 22)

As we continue our tour through the famous picture gallery, we come to a group of paintings with one central figure, Abraham. His example of faith is supreme in the Old Testament. "By faith Abraham obeyed when he was called . . . and he went out, not knowing where he was to go" (v. 8). God's call first came to Abraham when he was living at Ur, in Mesopotamia (cf. Acts 7:2–4); and to that call he gave immediate response. He left while the call was still ringing in his ears. And he did not have a road map in his pocket!

Although Abraham was reaching the land of promise, this was not his ultimate goal. He, as Isaac and Jacob did later, lived in tents as a stranger in a foreign land. Only the eternal city was his goal. He was looking forward to the city with solid foundations, "whose builder and maker is God" (v. 10).

Sarah also had faith. Even though advanced in years, "by faith . . . [she] received power to conceive" (v. 11). This is the rendering of the Revised Standard Version and other translations, but the New International Version and the New Revised Standard Version are quite different. (The difference depends on the reading(s) found in the Greek manuscripts.) Both Sarah and Abraham surely had faith in connection with Isaac's birth. Although at first Sarah laughed skeptically about having a child (Gen. 18:9–15), her laughter must have risen to faith long before Isaac's birth. Both Sarah and Abraham believed against all odds, trusting him "who had promised."

So from "one man [Abraham], and him as good as dead, were born descendants" (v. 12). Sarah no longer had the power to conceive, and Abraham no longer had the power to beget (cf. Rom. 4:19). Yet the certainty of God's promise set aside these obstacles. And as God had promised, their descendants became "as many as the stars of heaven and as the innumerable grains of sand by the seashore" (read Gen. 15:1–6; 22:15–18; cf. Isa. 51:2).

The author now pauses and reflects on the lives of the patriarchs. They lived in faith, they died in faith. They had in view a better life, a better resurrection (cf. 11:35). The author wants to imprint this on his readers' minds. They, too, as aliens in a foreign land, must live and die, still looking to the better things laid up for them in heaven.

The patriarchs did not die disappointed but with hope. They hailed the fulfillment of God's promise a long way off. This they could not "see," except by faith (cf. v. 1). Such faith caused them to acknowledge "that they were strangers and exiles on the earth" (see Gen. 23:4; 1 Chron. 29:15).

The lives of the patriarchs were consistent with their profession. "For people who speak thus make it clear that they are seeking a homeland" (v. 14). The point is that they could have gone back to Ur of the Chaldees, but they never did. They were lifelong pilgrims, who longed for "a better country . . . a heavenly one" (v. 16). With heaven as the patriarchs' goal, God proudly acknowledged them as his own. Indeed, God has his own city for them (cf. v. 10).

But faith will be tried. "By faith Abraham, when he was tested, offered up Isaac, and he who had received the promises was ready to offer up his only son" (v. 17). Twice this one verse refers to the "offering" of Isaac. Two different terms are used, explaining what actually happened. From Abraham's standpoint, he was going the limit in following God's commands—"he was ready to offer," "he was trying to offer" Isaac. From God's standpoint, though he had to intervene to stop the sacrifice, Abraham had truly obeyed him and had "offered" Isaac.

The strain on Abraham's faith was severe. In Isaac, the beloved son, were centered all the hopes and promises that God himself had made. How could he demand the slaying of Isaac? Abraham thought it through. "He considered that God was able to raise men even from the dead" (v. 19). Read Genesis 22:1–19. Picture Abraham as he goes to offer Isaac. He is not running joyfully and shouting "Hallelujah!" On the other hand, he is not hesitating and questioning God's love. No, he goes deliberately, obediently, in faith. And his great faith had a great reward. He received Isaac, so to speak, back from the dead.

The faith of Abraham was duplicated in the lives of his sons. Isaac and Jacob, by faith, looked toward the future and blessed their sons. Joseph, with faith, looked ahead to the exodus of Israel from Egypt. Yearning to be identified with God's people and God's promise, he gave directions concerning the removal of his bones (Gen. 50:24–25; cf. Exod. 13:19; Josh. 24:32).

The Faith of Moses (11:23—28)

The author next comes to the faith of Moses. Moses! Think of the metal of his faith, severely tested through long years, yet splendid and astonishing in result. As we have been doing, let us look at different scenes of his life as if depicted by paintings in a great gallery.

The faith of Moses begins with the faith of his parents. "By faith Moses, when he was born, was hid for three months by his parents" (v. 23). Exodus 2 records how the baby Moses was spared. Although Pharaoh had ordered the death of Hebrew newborn sons, Moses' parents were unafraid and ignored the king's edict. The author clearly wants to point out to his readers that faith does not fear or give in to despair.

So the first of this group of portraits is of the parents of Moses. The next portrait is of Moses as a young adult. "By faith Moses, when he was grown up, refused [despised] to be called the son of Pharaoh's daughter" (v. 24). To be the son of Pharaoh's daughter possibly means that Moses was heir to the throne of Egypt.

Moses, therefore, had to make a crisis decision. On one side was the court of Pharaoh, with its privileged position and immeasurable treasures. On the other side was "illtreatment with the people of God." To Moses' credit, by faith, he chose affliction rather than the temporary "pleasures of sin." He could not turn his back on God's people, which for him would have been "sin." He decided that "abuse suffered for the Christ" was "greater wealth" than all of Egypt's treasures. Think of the paradox: abuse for

Christ is wealth. Again, the author has his readers in mind. Moses, so to speak, suffered for God's Messiah, just as they are now expected to do (13:13). Moses can serve as their example of "looking ahead" to the eternal reward (cf. 13:14).

There are two other portraits of Moses, which we will look at briefly. "By faith he left Egypt, not being afraid of the anger of the king" (v. 27). Again, faith is unafraid. But did not Moses kill an Egyptian and escape to Midian for his life? (see Exod. 2:11–15). Yes, but by this time he had firmly decided to serve God. Having made that choice, he did not fear Pharaoh. In this sense Moses left Egypt by faith.

Acts 7:25 shows how Moses was thinking. He had made up his mind to be the deliverer of God's people. Yet when they were not ready for his leadership, and against all temptations to the contrary, Moses remained strong. "For he endured as seeing him who is invisible." The "for" is important. Moses was not afraid of Pharaoh, "for" he persevered in looking toward God. And all through those long years in Midian's desert, he persevered—until God finally called him to lead his people out of slavery. Faith holds on. It sees what others cannot see, even the Invisible God.

By faith Moses instituted the annual Passover observance. He "sprinkled the blood so that the Destroyer of the first-born might not touch them" (v. 28). God's judgment was about to fall on all of Egypt's first-born. Moses believed this and believed also that the only method of escape for Israel's first-born was by means of the sprinkling of lamb's blood. Moses and the people carefully obeyed God's commands, and the first-born of Israel were passed over unharmed.

Other Examples of Faith (11:29–38)

All other pictures in this great gallery continue to set forth what faith can accomplish. "By faith the people crossed the Red Sea as if on dry land" (v. 29). At first, the Israelites approached the Red Sea with enormous fear of the Egyptians (Exod. 14:10–14). Nevertheless, they obeyed God and passed safely through the sea.

Israel's faith was also demonstrated at Jericho. "By faith" the walls collapsed, "after they had been encircled seven days" (v. 30). Their maneuvers before a fortified city must have appeared ridiculous, but they gained the victory by following God's instructions (Josh. 6:1–21). Rahab, too, was saved by giving "friendly welcome" to the spies. She put her faith in the God who is "God in heaven above and on earth beneath" (Josh. 2:11).

What more can faith do? There are just too many pictures for the gallery. "Time would fail me," the author says, "to tell of Gideon, Barak, Samson, Jephthah, of David and Samuel and the prophets" (v. 32). The author has already singled out the faith of a number of extraordinary individuals. Now he adds to the list other names. Then, in a remarkably dramatic passage, he will move on to describe faith's heroic endurance under persecution.

Here Gideon is mentioned first, probably because of his stunning victory over the Midianites by his select 300, with their trumpets and clay jars (Judges 7). Barak and Deborah won the battle with Sisera and the Canaanites (Judges 4–5). Samson was the mighty warrior who killed a thousand Philistines and later died by pulling down the temple of Dagon (Judg. 15:9–17; 16:23–31). Jephthah and the men of Gilead prevailed over the Ammonites (Judges 11). David, Samuel, and the prophets are at the end of a list that could be much extended. Only to name their names recalls the glory that once was Israel's.

What can faith do? These heroes carried the day. Through faith they:

conquered kingdoms,
enforced justice,

received promises,
stopped the mouths of lions,
quenched raging fire,
escaped the edge of the sword,
won strength out of weakness,
became mighty in war,
put foreign armies to flight. (vv. 33–34)

Their faith subdued the enemy. It upheld justice. It saw promises fulfilled, (but not the Messianic promise).

What more can faith do? Look at Daniel in the lions' den (read Daniel 6). And look at Daniel's friends, Shadrach, Meshach, and Abednego. They will not bow before the Babylonian gods, and so they survive the "burning fiery furnace" into which they had been cast (Daniel 3). In addition, there are David (1 Sam. 18:11; 19:10–12) and Elijah (1 Kings 19) and Jeremiah (Jeremiah 26), all escaping death from the sword. In the days of Elijah and Elisha, even the dead were raised (1 Kings 17:17–24; 2 Kings 4:18–37). What is stronger than the power of faith?

But in those glorious days when faith triumphed in the lives of so many, others experienced apparent defeat. Some were thrown on the *tympanon!* The term refers to an instrument of torture, to a drum or rack on which the victim was stretched and beaten to death with clubs. "Others suffered mocking and scourging, and even chains and imprisonment" (v. 36; cf. 10:32–33).

The "faith of our fathers" sometimes means martyrdom. Often it means suffering. The author expects his readers to understand this. Will they, like their predecessors, choose the "better resurrection" instead of a resurrection to this life only?

The author now quickens his pace. Carefully, he builds up his phrases to a crescendo on the enormous suffering of the faithful.

They were stoned,
they were sawn in two,
they were killed with the sword;
they went about in skins of sheep and goats,
destitute,
afflicted,
ill-treated. (v. 37)

Zechariah was stoned to death under King Joash (2 Chron. 24:20–21; cf. Matt. 23:35). Jeremiah, tradition says, was stoned in Egypt. Isaiah, according to tradition, was sawn in two with a wooden saw. Others died by the sword; still others were forced from their homes to live a vagabond life.

Forlorn, oppressed, ill-treated! The author pauses to contemplate the horrid scene. Then, with moving eloquence, he interjects—the world was not worthy of them! Despised by the world as though they were nothing, they were only refugees. "Wandering over deserts and mountains and [dwelling] in dens and caves of the earth" (v. 38), they were living by faith. Truly, this earth was not their home.

Conclusion (11:39—40)

Now comes a concluding statement on the faith of our forefathers. "All these," the author says, "though well attested [in Scripture] by their faith, did not receive what was promised" (v. 39). By faith they waited and looked ahead, but they never received fulfillment.

God had a far-reaching plan in mind. He had foreseen "something better for us, that apart from us they should not be made perfect" (v. 40). Whatever is "better" is left unexpressed, or rather has already been expressed. Christ, whom the Old Testament exemplars did not know, has brought the better things. When he comes again, the faithful of both covenants will at last reach perfection together. "Beautiful Savior!"

QUESTIONS

1. How do the thoughts of 10:36 and 10:39 help us understand chapter 11? What are the historical circumstances of the readers that give rise to the great faith chapter?
2. Is 11:1 a full definition of faith? Explain the meaning of faith here.
3. Give the context of the statement, "Without faith it is impossible to please God" (11:6).
4. How is Abraham portrayed as a model for Christian pilgrims? Discuss the need for Christians to live in faith and to die in faith (cf. 11:13).
5. In what ways is Moses a splendid example of faith? Discuss and illustrate his endurance (11:27). What is said about Moses that would be especially applicable to the readers?
6. If faith produces great victories, does it also suffer apparent defeats? Give Biblical examples for your answer.

13

A Call to Perseverance

Hebrews 12:1—29

Let us run with perseverance.
HEBREWS 12:1

With chapter 12 we come to the lofty
climax of Hebrews, especially in
12:18–24. In these verses there is a final comparison and contrast of the two covenants.
The person of Christ and his priestly work
are now laid aside, but not entirely; for his
atoning blood still speaks eloquently in the
forgiveness of sins (12:24). Yet this message
of grace, God's last word from heaven, must
not be rejected (12:25–29) This is the letter's
stern, concluding warning against apostasy.

Having recounted faith's glorious deeds,
the author turns again to the situation of
his readers. "You have need of endurance
[hypomone]" (10:36), he has said. And now

he says again, in 12:1, that they must run the Christian race with all-out "endurance" (*hypomone*).

Notice what lies between these two appeals for endurance—the great faith chapter. The call for faith is a call for endurance. Chapter 11 is more than just a fine piece of writing. It is the sounding of the trumpets, the rolling of the drums, and the rallying of the troops for the decisive battle. Once again we see the author at his rhetorical best.

Looking to Jesus (12:1–3)

The first word in chapter 12 is a strong "therefore." The rousing exhortation continues. "Therefore, since we are surrounded by so great a cloud of witnesses . . . let us run with perseverance the race (Greek, *agon*) that is set before us" (v. 1). The *agon* is where the athletic contest took place, the arena of intense struggle and *agony*. In the Grecian games, the footrace was first in the order of the events and first in importance. It was deliberately designed as an endurance contest. For us, the race demands not brilliant starters but stouthearted plodders. It is a marathon, a race for a lifetime.

And we must strip down for the race. "Let us," the author says, including himself in the arena, "lay aside every weight." The race has eternal consequences, and no excess bodily weight or clothing must get in the way. What else hinders us? Sin! It "clings so closely." It deceives us, trips us up, and never lets us loose. But by God's grace we must cast aside all obstacles if we are to run this race.

Of course, we do not run the race unaided. All about us are "so great a cloud of witnesses"—the Old Testament heroes who have already had their faith commended by God (11:39). Having finished their course, they are now, figuratively speaking, the spectators who are cheering us on in our race of faith.

And there is another great source of encouragement. If we use the analogy we had before, we now enter another area of the portrait gallery; and of all things, here is a picture of Jesus—crucified. We have already examined many splendid portraits of faith (Hebrews 11), but Jesus' faith in suffering is the greatest of them all.

So we have to run our appointed race "looking to Jesus." We must look neither to the right nor to the left nor behind (cf. Luke 9:62) but only straight ahead to the goal. The author brings this out very forcefully. He uses a word for "look" (Greek, *aphorao*) in the special sense of looking away from everything else and fixing one's eyes on Jesus.

He is "the pioneer and perfecter of our faith." He is the "pioneer" (cf. 2:10) because he opened the way before us. He is the "perfecter" of our faith because he gave it its fullest expression. He perfectly modeled it. And here is something for us to remember. When we fix our gaze on the crucified Jesus, *then we discover the secret of running the race with endurance.*

Christ, our supreme example of faith and suffering, is the one toward whom we look. How was he able to finish his course? By focusing on "the joy" that later would be his, he "endured the cross" and despised its shame.

The horror of crucifixion was equaled only by the disgrace of it. It was a death for slaves and criminals. The victim was stripped of his clothing and fixed to the cross. Hanging helplessly, he was defenseless against the natural elements and the shame of exposure. But Jesus endured it. Paradoxically, he despised the shame by which he himself was shamed. And he realized his joy when he took his seat "at the right hand of the throne of God."

All through this passage the stress is on Jesus' example of endurance. "Consider him who endured from sinners such hostility against himself, so that you may not grow weary" (v. 3). If the readers have suffered bitter opposition from their enemies, they need only recall the cruel indignities that were heaped upon Christ. Comparing their light afflictions with his might well prevent them from dropping out of the race.

The Lesson of Discipline (12:4–11)

If they calculate correctly, the readers will know that their sufferings do not compare with his. They have suffered for Christ, and they must decide whether they will suffer for him even more (13:13). But they have not as yet resisted to the point of shedding their blood. Unlike Jesus, they have not died as martyrs.

The author speaks of their "struggle against sin." For all Christians sin is a real struggle. But the thought here is not so much of the inner conflict with sin but of its outer opposition. The battle against everything opposed to Christ is personified as a "struggle against sin."

But when suffering comes, it is easy to think that God has forsaken us. Actually, just the reverse is true. God is a gracious Father who stands with his children in adversity. Indeed, he uses such adverse experiences to discipline his children for their good.

"Discipline" is the key word in these verses, concerning which the author stresses three things.

1. God's Word. "Have you forgotten," the author asks, "the exhortation which addresses you as sons?—'My son, do not regard lightly the discipline of the Lord, nor lose courage when you are punished by him'" (v. 5). The quotation is from Proverbs 3:11–12. Notice that the words of Scripture are called an "exhortation."

The child of God often displays one or other of two attitudes toward discipline. On one hand, he may look upon it lightly and disregard it. He does not understand that God disciplines his own. When trouble comes, he does not think it through and see God at work in it. On the other hand, he may be so discouraged by hardship that he quits the race and falls away from the Lord entirely.

2. God's love. The quotation from Proverbs continues: "For the Lord disciplines him whom he loves, and chastises every son whom he receives" (v. 6). We must remember that God is first and foremost the God of love. If we as his children suffer persecution or whatever, this may mean only that God loves us dearly.

3. God's purpose. With the end of the quotation, the author begins to explain God's purpose in discipline. The suffering, which the readers were presently enduring, must be viewed as divine discipline. Sonship involves discipline; otherwise, they would be "illegitimate children and not sons." The principle is a long-standing one. "As a man disciplines his son, the LORD your God disciplines you" (Deut. 8:5).

The point is further elaborated. "Besides this, we have had earthly fathers to discipline us and we respected them. Shall we not much more be subject to the Father of spirits and live?" (v. 9). Earthly fathers discipline us, sometimes quite imperfectly, and yet do we not respect them? If so, then how much more respect—and submission—is due to "the Father of spirits" (our spiritual Father), who disciplines us that we might live forever?

Yes, human fathers "disciplined us for a short time as seemed best to them, but he disciplines us for our good, in order that we may share his holiness" (v. 10 NRSV). Earthly discipline is temporary and too often whimsical. But God's discipline is never arbitrary. His final goal for us is that we may share eternally the holiness of God himself (cf. Acts 14:22).

So we have to keep in mind God's ultimate purpose for us. "For the moment all discipline seems painful rather than pleasant. Later it yields the peaceful fruit of righteousness to those who have been trained by it" (v. 11). Of course, no one at the moment enjoys discipline. When we suffer, we hurry to God and ask that the pain be taken away. But we must trust him and know that our Father is training us by means of discipline. In due time, it will bring forth fruit. Its result, in contrast to pain, will be the peace of an upright life.

Encouraging Others (12:12–17)

We have been noticing that the author's custom is to state ahead of time the themes he plans to pursue. The fifth of these "announcement themes" appears in 12:11—THE PEACEFUL FRUIT OF RIGHTEOUSNESS. This is the last of these themes, which in a few words summarizes the remainder of the author's letter.

"Therefore lift your drooping hands and strengthen your weak knees, and make straight paths for your feet [cf. Isa. 35:3; Prov. 4:26], so that what is lame may not be put out of joint but rather be healed" (vv. 12–13). The exhortation shifts a little and is directed to those who are more mature in the congregation. They are to be strong, go straight ahead, and not lose heart in their difficult circumstances. By doing this they will be able to help the "lame" among them who are near fatigue on their heaven-set journey. The strong must always be aware of and help the needs of the weak (cf. Rom. 15:1).

Reference to the "lame" may point again to some of the readers who are in danger of falling away (cf. 3:12; 6:4–8; 10:25–31). This becomes clearer in the verses that follow. "Strive for peace with [everyone NRSV], and for the holiness without which no one will see the Lord" (v. 14). "Peace" is an echo of the theme announced in verse 11. "Holiness," that is, living a holy life, must be the one characteristic of the Christian whose goal is to be with God (cf. v. 10; Matt. 5:8).

Fearing that some of them might fall as apostates, the author now directs three warnings to the congregation.

1. "See to it that no one fail to obtain the grace of God" (v. 15). "See to it" is the translation of a term related to the word *episkopos* ("bishop" or "overseer"), but what is applied to church leaders elsewhere is here addressed to all members of the congregation. Each one has the responsibility to see about others. Today is the day of salvation, and we must see that no one in the end is excluded from the rich provisions of God's grace.

2. "[See to it] that no 'root of bitterness' spring up and cause trouble." The author fears that a bitter or poisonous root (cf. Deut. 29:18) might spring up among them and infect the whole congregation. They would then become "defiled" and lose their "holiness" so essential for seeing God.

3. "[See to it] that no one be immoral or irreligious like Esau" (v. 16). According to 13:4, immorality seems to have been a problem for some in the congregation. Esau is typical of the irreligious or unspiritual person. To him belonged the rights of the elder son, which he quickly forfeited "for a single meal" (see Gen. 25:29–34). What was he thinking about? His future blessings? The promises God had made to Abraham and Isaac? No! Only his momentary hunger pangs!

Once Esau had sold his birthright, the deed could not be undone. "Afterward, when he desired to inherit the blessing, he was rejected" (v. 17). The sad story of Isaac and Jacob, and of Jacob's receiving Isaac's blessing, is recorded in Genesis 27. When the blessing was pronounced, it could not be changed. In this sense "[Esau] found no chance to repent, though he sought it with tears." This does not mean that he was unable to repent of his sins. The meaning is, rather, that Esau had foolishly placed himself in a position where no change could be made concerning his inheritance.

The warning is sharp to those in danger of apostasy, lest they lose God's gracious promises (cf. 11:39; 12:22–29) and fall into ruin.

Sinai and Zion (12:18–24)

We now begin the rhetorical climax of Hebrews. It is the grand finale of this "little masterpiece"—glorious and triumphant. In one majestic contrast-picture, the author lays out before his readers the vast difference between the old and the new covenants, between Sinai and Zion. The call is for them to compare the wonder of their present privileges with what Israel had. They must understand that there is no alternative for them but Christ; that to be in him is to experience the greatest blessings God has bestowed on mankind. How can those who have been to Mount Zion desire to return to Mount Sinai?

The two pictures of contrast are introduced with opposite expressions: "For you have not come" (v. 18), "But you have come" (v. 22). The reference is back to the time when the readers first became Christians. At their conversion they did not come to Sinai, to "a blazing fire, and darkness, and gloom, and a tempest, and the sound of a trumpet" (vv. 18–19).

The forbidding scene is described in Exodus 19:18–19. "And Mount Sinai was wrapped in smoke, because the LORD descended upon it in fire . . . and the whole mountain quaked greatly. And as the sound of the trumpet grew louder and louder, Moses spoke, and God answered him in thunder." (For the whole scene, read Exod. 19–20 and Deut. 4–5.)

The voice of God frightened the people and caused them to "beg that not another word be spoken to them" (NRSV). They were afraid not only of God but of his stern command that if even a straying animal touched the mountain, it should be stoned. "Indeed, so terrifying was the sight that Moses said, 'I tremble with fear'" (v. 21).

The author's grim picture of Mount Sinai emphasizes how distant and unapproachable God was under the old covenant. But now, through Christ and faith in him, how wonderfully different everything is. "But you have come," the author says, "to Mount Zion and to the city of the living God, the heavenly Jerusalem" (v. 22).

The reference is not at all to an earthly Zion, but to the heavenly city built by God. Christians stand directly before this city. They belong to heaven, though they have not literally entered into it. Still they have to persevere, still they must "seek the city which is to come" (13:14). Theirs is the time of fulfillment but not yet of consummation.

Since a city has inhabitants, the author proceeds to enumerate those of the heavenly city, including the "innumerable angels in festal gathering, and the assembly of the first-born who are enrolled in heaven" (vv. 22–23). Angels were present at Mount Sinai, a scene of terror, but in the heavenly city ten thousands of angels throng about God with joyous worship as at a religious festival.

But does "the assembly of the first-born" also refer to the angels? No! "Assembly" is the normal term for "church" (*ekklesia*), and nowhere else in Scripture are the angels called the "first-born." And why would they be spoken of as "enrolled in heaven"? It is much more likely that the "first-born ones" are believers and that the author is describing the heavenly city as it ultimately will be. Right now we are not there. One day we will enjoy the full privileges of citizens in that city. In the meantime, it is enough that we are heirs (1:14; cf. Rom. 8:17). Our names are written down on the census roll in heaven (see Luke 10:20; Phil. 4:3; Rev. 21:27).

In the celestial city, of course, God is there. He is described either as "a judge who is God of all" or as "God who is judge of all." (Either translation is possible; the former follows the literal word order in Greek.) He is Judge and Lord of all beings, human and angelic. And the heavenly city includes, besides, "the spirits of the righteous made perfect" (NRSV). The departed dead are spiritual beings who lived their lives in righteousness. They have now been "perfected." In death they have finally arrived at their goal.

So here we are before the city of God. Who else is there? Jesus! We have come "to Jesus, the mediator of a new covenant," and to his "sprinkled blood that speaks more graciously [literally, better] than the blood of Abel" (v. 24). Abel's blood cried for vengeance and retribution, Jesus' blood calls for grace and pardon. For special emphasis, Jesus is placed last in the listing of the city's population. Indeed, the statement here about Jesus summarizes much of the message of Hebrews—Jesus is the mediator of the new covenant, and his blood speaks graciously in forgiveness.

"Let Us Be Grateful" (12:25–29)

Sinai or Zion? Which will it be? This grand section of contrasts continues and rises to its conclusion. Again, the readers are warned against their falling away. "See that you do not refuse [or disregard] him who is speaking." Notice the connection. The blood of Christ speaks [forgiveness] (v. 24), the voice of God speaks [in the gospel] (v. 25). If the Israelites failed to escape when God warned them at Sinai—there and on countless other occasions they refused to hear God's voice—how can we escape if we disregard the one who now warns from heaven? What escape is possible for those who reject "such a great salvation"?

Then, God's voice in the wilderness "shook the earth." Now God has promised, "Yet once more I will shake not only the earth but also the heaven" (cf. Hag. 2:6). God shakes things. "Yet once more," in a near day, he will shake everything. The whole, visible, created universe will pass away. With such an upheaval foreseen and certain, why hang on to what cannot last? That is precisely the predicament of the original readers. If they opt for the old covenant, with its earthly sanctuary and sacrificial system, they will end up with nothing!

The old universe will perish, but there is another, heavenly universe which can never be moved. "Therefore," the author entreats, "let us be grateful for receiving a kingdom that cannot be shaken" (v. 28). If ever there is a verse in the Bible that says "count your blessings," this is it. Let us be thankful for our many blessings in Christ, and let us be thankful for our privileged membership in the heavenly kingdom. It alone is unshakable and will endure in power and glory even after Christ returns.

We have much to be grateful for, and therefore, the author urges, "Let us offer to God acceptable worship, with reverence and awe." Worship and gratitude go together. A grateful heart flows forth with adoring worship.

The author ends his thought, however, with a note of stern caution. Acceptable worship must be "with reverence and awe"—the opposite of presumptuous familiarity—"for our God is a consuming fire" (v. 29). In 10:27 the author has spoken of a "fury of fire" and in 6:8 of land which bears "thorns and thistles . . . [whose] end is to be burned." It is significant that in both of these passages the subject is "apostasy." So here the description of God as a "consuming fire" (cf. Deut. 4:18) is yet another warning against those who would turn away as apostates.

Those who are tempted to turn back must be warned, yet in these verses there is a vibrant message of hope. God is indeed a devouring fire, but he is also the God of grace and the God of great promises. For Jesus Christ is the center of it all, and it is his blood that offers pardon. This is the message of the gospel. And whenever warnings appear in Hebrews, they are from a Father who loves us, who speaks to us through his terrors in order that we may not disregard his merciful voice.

QUESTIONS

1. How is the exhortation to run with endurance (12:1) connected with chapter 11? What are the things that might hinder in the race? What is the secret of running the race successfully?
2. What is the not-to-be-forgotten exhortation in 12:5? Discuss God's love and purpose in discipline for the readers and for us.
3. What are the specific instructions given to the congregation as a whole in 12:12–17? Recount the sad lesson of Esau.
4. Describe the climactic scene of contrast between Mount Sinai and Mount Zion (12:18–29). What does this all mean?
5. Who are represented as citizens of the heavenly city? How have Christians come, and not yet come, to this city? Is *your* name written there?
6. Above all things, what are Christians to be grateful for (12:28)? In gratitude, what are we to offer God? Review Hebrews and make a list of passages concerning worship. What can such a list teach us?

14

A Call to Pilgrims

Hebrews 13:1 — 25

Here we have no lasting city, but we seek
the city which is to come.
HEBREWS 13:14

With the concluding verses of chapter 12, the author brings his letter to an eloquent climax. Which will it be for his readers, the gloom and darkness of Sinai or the joy and hope of Zion? Is it to be a covenant that required the people to stand back or a covenant, based on Christ's sacrifice, in which believers are encouraged to draw near and offer acceptable worship to God?

Chapter 13 marks a change in tone. A letter that has brought us to the heights of the glory of Jesus Christ ends with down-to-earth instructions. But that is the very nature of this letter—always exalting Christ yet filled with needed exhortations. And as we come to the close of Hebrews, let us remember that we will truly profit from our study if, by God's help, we are able to put it in our daily lives.

Practical Exhortations (13:1—6)

The chapter begins with a series of exhortations. Since love is so basic, it is first on the list. "Let brotherly love continue." The Greek word for "brotherly love" is *philadelphia,* a special word in the New Testament for love of brothers and sisters in Christ. In 2:11–12 Jesus consciously identifies himself with his brothers, which is the basis of Christian brotherhood. As the readers had displayed love toward one another in the past (6:10; 10:33–34), so now they are urged to maintain that love.

One practical expression of love is hospitality. "Do not neglect to show hospitality to strangers" (v. 2). Hospitality was regarded as an honored virtue in the ancient world. Because Jesus taught the reception of strangers (Matt. 25:35), hospitality became a distinguishing mark for his disciples and was to be extended especially to traveling Christians and evangelists (Rom. 12:13; 1 Peter 4:9; 3 John 5–8).

Hospitality has its rewards, for "some have entertained angels" without knowing it. The reference is probably to the wonderful occasion when Abraham greeted and entertained three mysterious guests, who later turned out to be angels (see Gen. 18:1–19:1). What a beautiful thought: visitors in one's home may actually be angels.

Another expression of love, also exalted by Jesus (Matt. 25:36), is the care of prisoners. "Remember those who are in prison, as though in prison with them" (v. 3). Timothy had recently been released (13:23), and the readers are to see about the needs of others who remained in prison. Strangers might visibly appear at their doors for help, but prisoners were out of sight and must not be forgotten.

"As though in prison with them" suggests the Golden Rule (Matt. 7:12), the disposition Christians should always have toward others. A similar spirit must be shown to those who are mistreated, the author says, "as if you yourselves were suffering" (NIV).

Brotherly love that is genuine rules out marital infidelity. "Let marriage be held in honor among all, and let the marriage bed be undefiled" (v. 4). Although Jesus taught self-denial, he was not an ascetic. To deny human sexuality or to forbid marriage (cf. 1 Tim. 4:3) is not to be confused with true spirituality. To the contrary, marriage is to be honored. But sexual promiscuity will bring judgment that comes from God himself.

Selfishness may express itself in immorality or in greed. "Keep your life free from love of money, and be content with what you have" (v. 5). Living by faith demands a different attitude toward earthly things. Money is not an end in itself, and craving for it causes many pitfalls. The admonition here is very similar to Paul's pointed instructions about wealth and contentment (see 1 Tim. 6:6–10; cf. Phil. 4:11).

But does contentment mean absence of ambition and economic stagnation? The answer is that contentment is an attitude of mind made possible by a determined trust in God. And what has God said? "I will never fail you nor forsake you" (v. 5). This promise was first made to Israel and to Joshua when Moses was about to be parted from them and then restated to Joshua as he was beginning his victorious campaigns (Deut. 31:6, 8; Josh. 1:5).

Because of God's unfailing presence, the believer can courageously say, "The Lord is my helper, I will not be afraid; what can man do to me?" The words, from Psalm 118:6, apply with special force to the readers who were face to face with persecution. If they maintain God as their strength, that will be enough to carry them through.

Warning against False Teachings (13:7—16)

A new section begins, stressing that the readers should continue in the word as it was originally taught. "Remember your leaders, those who spoke to you the word of God; consider the outcome of their life, and imitate their faith" (v. 7). The author clearly is thinking of their former leaders, probably those who had established the congregation. They had spoken God's message, and their way of life was faithful to the end. Their lives had set a recent example of faith worthy of imitation.

Next comes the most familiar verse in Hebrews. It reads, if translated literally: "Jesus Christ yesterday and today the same and forever" (v. 8). Christ is changeless, yes, but notice the emphasis—today he is the same. Christ is the same today, and today his gospel is the same as it was first preached to the readers.

Therefore, that gospel must ever be held on to and not supplanted by other teachings. "Do not be carried away by all kinds of strange teachings" (v. 9 NRSV). The multiplicity of teachings is in contrast to the one, authentic teaching already delivered. They were "strange," that is, they were foreign to the central nature of Christianity.

A clue about these teachings is given in the rest of the verse: "It is well that the heart be strengthened by grace, not by foods, which have not benefited their adherents." Look at the big difference between "foods" and "grace."

On one hand are those who think that foods—either eating or not eating them—bring one close to God (see 1 Cor. 8:8; Rom. 14:17). The author is emphatic that they do not. He has already said that "foods and drinks and various ablutions [washings NIV]" (9:10) cannot deal with the conscience. Here the thought is similar. On the other hand is God's grace. It can strengthen the heart. It can vitally affect the conscience and bring a person near God.

And notice that God's grace connects directly with what follows. "We have an altar from which those who serve the tent have no right to eat" (v. 10). "We have" is first in the sentence and is emphatic. What we Christians have is in sharp contrast with what "those who serve the tent" do not have. The tent is the tabernacle of Israel's desert wandering. Those who serve it are the Levitical priests, as the next verse goes on to imply.

But what does the author mean by saying that Christians have an altar? Clearly, he does not mean that we have a material altar on earth. Rather, again, he is using language of analogy and comparison. In 8:2, for example, he has described Christ's priestly ministry in heaven as a service in the "true tent," which is not literally a tent in any sense. So here he is speaking figuratively. "Look to heaven," he says. "Our altar is there. And look what has been laid on the altar. Christ! He has been offered for our sins once for all!"

The author goes on to explain. "For the bodies of those animals whose blood is brought into the sanctuary by the high priest as a sacrifice for sin are burned outside the camp" (v. 11). The reference is to the Day of Atonement, when the high priest officiated. On this occasion the flesh of the animals sacrificed was not to be eaten. The priests who tended the altar normally ate of the sacrifices, but not on that day. Instead, the animal bodies were carried outside the camp and burned (Lev. 16:27).

The point is that Christians do have an altar, and it is the sacrifice of Christ. What earthly altar can compare with this? We Christians, by God's grace, can partake of it, but others are excluded. Just as the Levitical priests were forbidden to eat of the animals slain on Atonement Day, so anyone who would cling to Judaism cannot share in the blessings of Christ's sacrifice.

As the animals were burned outside the camp, "so Jesus also suffered outside the gate in order to sanctify the people through his own blood" (v. 12). Sanctification by his blood echoes a predominant theme (9:12–14; 10:10, 14). Jesus, rejected and despised by his own people, died outside the walls of Jerusalem. "Outside," for both author and readers, has special significance.

Now comes the crux of the whole matter. "Therefore let us go forth to him outside the camp, bearing abuse for him" (v. 13). The language is strong: "Let us go *out* to him *outside*." Out! Out! And notice "outside the camp" (v. 11), "outside the gate" (v. 12), and "outside the camp" (v. 13). Condemned as a blasphemer, crucified like a slave, Jesus died outside the city, where law-breakers were punished. It was for him the ultimate reproach (cf. 12:2; Gal. 3:13).

The appeal is forcefully direct. Including himself in the exhortation, the author is saying: "Let us go to Christ outside Jerusalem. He did not die inside but outside. Outside the city, outside the center of Judaism, that is where Christ is and that is where atonement is. The old sacrificial order has passed away. You must decide for Christ and go to him, even if it ends in suffering."

Shame and abuse were to be theirs, if they were to follow him. But why not? "For here [on earth] we have no lasting city, but we seek the city which is to come" (v. 14). The verse is a key verse in Hebrews, one that we should all try to memorize. Stated so simply, it is a gentle reminder of who we really are as Christians. We are just pilgrims passing through. Like our forefathers of faith, we, too, as "strangers and foreigners" on earth, are "seeking a homeland" (11:13–16; cf. 11:10).

The readers have been summoned to forsake Judaism, and now they are summoned to the pathway of pilgrimage. Indeed, their call to be pilgrims is so fundamental. Look at the connecting "for." The author is saying: "Let us go to Christ outside the camp. Let us bear his stigma. *For* here cities disappear, but God's city [still future for believers] remains. Let us be like pilgrims and consciously seek that city."

In the meantime, as we journey toward the heavenly city, we should be offering spiritual sacrifices. "Through him then let us continually offer up a sacrifice of praise to God" (v. 15). "Through him" is first for emphasis. As worshipers are brought near to God through him (7:25), as sin is put away by (literally, through) the sacrifice of himself (9:26), so now worship is to be done through him. A heart strengthened by grace will continue to pour forth praise, gratefully acknowledging him with the lips.

In addition to thanksgiving, there are the never-to-be-neglected sacrifices of good deeds. "Do not neglect to do good and share what you have, for such sacrifices are pleasing to God" (v. 16). "To share what you have" translates the meaningful New Testament word, *koinonia*. This overlaps with doing good, and here refers especially to doing good to one's fellow Christians.

Final Words (13:17—25)

Although arranged under a new heading, verse 17 connects immediately with the previous paragraph. "Remember your leaders" (v. 7), "obey your leaders" (v. 17). The full command is "Obey your leaders and submit to them." Surely, this must be understood in context. Verses 7 and 17 serve as brackets and in between is the strong warning against "strange teachings" (vv. 9–14). The readers are to remember their former leaders because they had first taught them God's word. They are to obey their present leaders because they, too, stand for the word of God. So obey/submit does not demand blind obedience to any and every leader/teacher.

The author says three more things about the present leaders of this congregation.

1. They watch. Instead of saying to the readers "they watch over you," the author says beautifully, "they are keeping watch over your souls" (cf. 6:19; 10:39). The figure is that of the shepherd, overseeing and protecting the flock.

2. They will give account. The thought is not that they are "accountable" for the actions of others but, rather, that they must answer to God for the way in which they have served as shepherds. Accountable to God! What shall it be on that day when the books are opened?

3. They should serve with joy. "Let them do this joyfully, and not sadly" (literally, "not with groaning"). The implication is that the present leaders were overburdened with the care of the congregation. Certainly so, if some of the members were in danger of abandoning their faith and returning to Judaism.

On the other hand, by remembering the sound teaching of their leaders, that would bring them joy instead of grief. And the further thought here is that sighing and groaning leadership would in no way commend the condition of the congregation.

Next comes the request for the readers' prayers. "Pray for us" in verse 18 becomes in verse 19, "I urge you the more earnestly to do this." Explaining why he seeks their prayers, in effect the author says: "Remember and obey your leaders, pray for me. I don't want you to misunderstand my intentions in writing this letter. I have a good conscience and I want to do the right thing."

The request is especially for earnest prayer, that the author might rejoin the congregation very soon. The readers are to be "more earnest" in their prayers, just as they are to be "more earnest" in giving heed to God's word (2:1). The author's hope to be restored to the readers reminds them that he would much rather be there and deliver his message personally. Even though this letter may be anonymous to us, it certainly was not anonymous to its original readers.

The author, who has asked for their prayers, lovingly prays for them. "Now may the God of peace who brought again from the dead our Lord Jesus, the great shepherd of the sheep, by the blood of the eternal covenant, equip you with everything good that you may do his will, working in you that which is pleasing in his sight, through Jesus Christ; to whom be the glory for ever and ever. Amen" (vv. 20–21).

What an expressive and eloquent benediction, perhaps the most beautiful one in the New Testament (cf. Jude 24–25). The emphasis of the prayer is on God, on what he can do and what his will is, all to his glory. Too often our prayers focus more on ourselves than on God and the working of his will.

God is described in the prayer as the God who gives "peace." Peace in general refers to well-being or health, but often in the New Testament it is the practical equivalent of salvation (Acts 10:36; Eph. 2:17). God also is the one who raised "our Lord Jesus." He who brought Christ back from the dead is a Mighty God. There is nothing he cannot do to strengthen his people and answer their prayers.

Jesus, the shepherd of the sheep (cf. John 10:11–18), recalls the leaders as shepherds in verse 17. But he is the Great Shepherd, all others are underlings (cf. 1 Peter 5:4). The author says this in the strongest way possible, similar to John 10:11. Translated literally, the expressions are parallel:

> The shepherd, the good one. (John 10:11)
> The shepherd, the great one. (Heb. 13:20)

Reference to "the blood of the eternal covenant" points back to the central theme of the grand middle section in this letter (8:1–10:18). Christ's blood atones for sin and confirms the new covenant which promises forgiveness. It is a covenant that is eternally valid (cf. 9:12).

The main thrust of the prayer is not that they may have everything, but that the readers may have everything to do God's will. Earlier, they have been called to endurance in order to do his will (10:36). Here the prayer is that they may be equipped to do it, God accomplishing his purpose in them through Jesus Christ. And to the Almighty God belong praise and glory "for ever and ever."

Only a few other matters remain in verses 22–25. For all practical purposes the letter ends with the prayer. Mention is made of Timothy, of travel plans, and of special greetings. These items add a bit more insight into the historical situation of the people addressed, about whom we would like to learn so much more. Things of this kind appear typically at the end of Greek letters. The final words convey the blessing of God's grace upon all who read the letter.

Verse 22 contains one last plea: "I appeal to you, brethren, bear with my word of exhortation, for I have written to you briefly." When the author says "bear with" my message, he does not mean that the readers should "tolerate" or "endure" it. Rather, knowing that they might take exception to it, he is begging that they might open their hearts and "receive" it.

And receive it they should! But did they? In that far-off century, when they assembled together, when they heard the reading of this letter for the first time, what did they think? Did they welcome it? Did they turn from their spiritual lethargy and gratefully acknowledge Christ and his sacrifice? And would they bear abuse for him? Looking back, we can only hope that their letter restored them to the love they had at first.

We have been reading this remarkable letter, and we have been sitting at the feet of one of the great teachers in the early church. The readers' challenges and struggles have become ours. We may not know where they lived or much about them. But when, by God's grace, heaven becomes our eternal possession, hopefully we will be able to meet them (and their teacher) and tell them how much this letter has meant to us all. And surely, in that unshakable kingdom, we will join the hosts of its heavenly citizens, to praise and thank the God of all and our Lord Jesus!

> Beautiful Savior! Lord of all nations!
> Son of God and Son of Man.
> Glory and Honor, Praise, adoration
> Now and forever more be thine.

QUESTIONS

1. If Hebrews is characteristically rhetorical, why do you think it ends with practical exhortations? Which of these exhortations do you need to especially remember?
2. Give the context of "Jesus Christ is the same yesterday and today and forever" (13:8). Show how this is directly connected with verses 7 and 9.
3. Why does the author of Hebrews want his readers to remember their leaders (13:7, 17)? Are all leaders to be followed, no matter what?
4. What is the altar that Christians have that others cannot share in (13:10)?
5. Explain the exhortation in 13:13. What does this say about the purpose of this letter?
6. Explain 13:14 as a special call for Christian pilgrims. How can Christians be not of the world and yet have a mission in the world?

For Further Reading

A List for the General Reader

Brown, Raymond. *The Message of Hebrews: Christ above All.* The Bible Speaks Today Series. Downers Grove, Ill.: InterVarsity, 1982.

Bruce, Alexander Balmain. *The Epistle to the Hebrews: The First Apology for Christianity.* Edinburgh: T. & T. Clark, 1899. Reprint, Minneapolis: Klock & Klock Christian, 1980.

Ellingworth, Paul. *The Epistle to the Hebrews.* London: Epworth, 1991.

Gooding, David. *An Unshakeable Kingdom: The Letter to the Hebrews for Today.* Grand Rapids: Eerdmans, 1989.

Guthrie, Donald. *The Letter to the Hebrews.* Tyndale New Testament Commentaries. Grand Rapids: Eerdmans, 1983.

Hagner, Donald A. *Hebrews.* New International Biblical Commentary. Peabody, Mass.: Hendrickson, 1990.

Lane, William L. *Hebrews: A Call to Commitment.* Peabody, Mass.: Hendrickson, 1985.

Lightfoot, Neil R. *Jesus Christ Today: A Commentary on the Book of Hebrews.* Grand Rapids: Baker, 1976. Reprint, Abilene, Tex.: Bible Guides, 1989.

Stedman, Ray C. *Hebrews.* The IVP New Testament Commentary Series. Downers Grove, Ill.: InterVarsity, 1992.

Stibbs, Alan M. *So Great Salvation: The Meaning and Message of the Letter to the Hebrews.* Exeter: Paternoster, 1970.

Thompson, James W. *The Letter to the Hebrews.* Austin, Tex.: R. B. Sweet, 1971.

Wilson, R. McL. *Hebrews.* New Century Bible Commentary. Grand Rapids: Eerdmans, 1987.

Neil R. Lightfoot (Ph.D., Duke University) serves as Frank Pack Distinguished Professor of New Testament at Abilene Christian University in Abilene, Texas. He is the author of several books, including *How We Got the Bible*.